# Market Failure

## Market-Based Electricity is Killing Nuclear Power

*Edward Kee*
*CEO, Nuclear Economics Consulting Group*

NECG

Washington, DC

# Market Failure

Edward Kee

NECG (Nuclear Economics Consulting Group)
PO Box 2454
Alexandria, VA 22301
USA
www.nuclear-economics.com

The author and publisher are not responsible for websites
(or their content) owned by others.

Paperback Version
First Edition:  January 2021
ISBN 13: 978-1-7323644-1-7

Market Failure

# PREFACE

The biggest threat faced by nuclear power is from a market approach to the electricity industry. Electricity industry reforms have led to the early closure of existing nuclear power plants and stopped new nuclear power development.

In the US, 6,778 MWe of operating nuclear power plant capacity was closed early between 2013 and 2020, an additional 9,162 MWe of operating nuclear power plant capacity is scheduled to close early by the end of 2025, and more US merchant nuclear plants face financial issues that may lead them to close early.

In the market approach to electricity, short-term electricity market prices set the value of commodity electricity, electricity prices define power plant value, and private companies develop and own power plants based on financial returns. This market approach leads to less nuclear power, with the loss of the considerable public benefits that nuclear power provides.

Economists call this market failure.

This book includes information on the nuclear power and electricity industries, market failure in the nuclear power industry, and some ideas about resolving this market failure.

The ideas in this book were developed in client engagements, published articles, presentations, discussions with industry experts, and Nuclear Economics Consulting Group (NECG) Commentaries. NECG's Affiliated Experts and other colleagues provided helpful comments and suggestions on the concepts in this book. Jamie Boucher helped me understand how those outside the nuclear power industry view this book's concepts.

Any errors or oversights in this book are mine. Please send any comments, suggestions, or other ideas related to this book to marketfailure@nuclear-economics.com.

Edward Kee
Washington, DC
January 2021

# CONTENTS

# Market Failure

*"Nuclear power plants
are getting killed in US
markets."*

David Roberts - *How to Save the Failing Nuclear Power
Plants that Generate Half of America's Clean Electricity*[1]

Market Failure

# INTRODUCTION

*"...there is no sensible alternative to nuclear energy"*

James Lovelock - *Nuclear Energy for the 21<sup>st</sup> Century*[2]

Nuclear power is too important to be left to the market.

The biggest threat faced by nuclear power is from a market approach to the electricity industry. Electricity industry reforms and a market approach to the electricity industry have led to the premature closure of existing nuclear power plants and the failure to develop and build new nuclear power projects.

The US market approach to electricity and nuclear power led to the early and permanent closure of 6,778 MWe of US operating nuclear power plant capacity between 2013 and 2020, the scheduled closure of another 9,162 MWe of US operating nuclear power plant capacity by the end of 2025, and financial issues at other operating nuclear power plants that may mean even more early closures.

1

A market approach to electricity will mean fewer nuclear power plants. The public good from these missing nuclear power plants will be lost. When market outcomes reduce public good, economists call this market failure.

This book explains why nuclear power matters, nuclear power, electricity and electricity reform, the market failure concept, real-world experience with nuclear power, and how nuclear power market failure can be resolved.

The following is a summary of the chapters in this book.

*Why Nuclear Power Matters* outlines my view of the valuable attributes that should make nuclear power a preferred electricity source.

*Nuclear Power* provides information on the nuclear power industry. It explains industry terminology, nuclear power project development phases, costs of building and operating nuclear power plants, operating modes, industry organization, business models, and key industry risks and issues.

*Electricity* provides information on the electricity industry. Nuclear power plants, almost exclusively, are special-purpose machines that generate electricity. The value of electricity determines the value of nuclear power. The electricity industry has a traditional approach that has been in place for almost a century, and a new industry approach developed during electricity industry reforms started in the 1990s.

*Market Failure* explains market failure, which is when private companies acting in markets fail to maximize the public good. This book is about market failure for nuclear power from a market-based approach to electricity.

*Nuclear Power in the Real World* provides detailed information on nuclear power in the US, the UK, Canada, France, and China. In these five countries, differences in electricity and nuclear power industry approaches lead to very different nuclear power outcomes. This chapter provides clear evidence of market failure.

*What Can be Done?* outlines some actions that could help resolve market failure for nuclear power.

*A Call to Action* explains the urgency and importance of recognizing market failure for nuclear power and taking action to stop it.

Edward Kee

# WHY NUCLEAR POWER MATTERS

*"Nuclear power is carbon-free, technologically feasible, scalable, and economical."*

MIT - *The Urgent Need for Increased Nuclear Power*[3]

This chapter explains why nuclear power provides valuable attributes and benefits that should make it a preferred electricity source.

Nuclear power is the only feasible technology to replace combustion-based electricity generation. Nuclear power generates carbon-free electricity (i.e., like renewable generation) from compact, reliable, and dispatchable power plants (i.e., like combustion-based generation).

# Nuclear Power Attributes

### *Reliable*

Nuclear power is the most reliable electricity generation technology as measured by capacity factor. The capacity factor is the electricity generated by a power plant divided by the electricity generated if the plant operates at maximum output, typically measured over a year.

Table 1 shows that the 2019 US nuclear power capacity factor is much higher than the capacity factor for other generating technologies. World nuclear power capacity factor in 2019 was 82.5%.[4]

Nuclear power plants have a high capacity factor because they are usually operated at full output when available, referred to as base-load operating mode.

Nuclear power plants continue to operate reliably during extreme weather events, at night (i.e., when solar power is not available), and in low wind conditions. Nuclear power plants do not face fuel delivery disruptions (e.g., natural gas pipeline problems or curtailment).

### Table 1 - US Capacity Factors for 2019

| | |
|---|---|
| Nuclear | 93.5% |
| Geothermal | 74.4% |
| Natural gas combined cycle | 56.8% |
| Coal | 47.5% |
| Hydroelectric | 39.1% |
| Wind | 34.8% |
| Solar (photovoltaic) | 24.5% |
| Solar (thermal) | 21.2% |
| Natural gas steam turbine | 14.3% |
| Natural gas combustion turbine | 11.8% |
| Petroleum combustion turbine | 1.1% |

*Source: U.S. EIA Electric Power Monthly*

### *Flexible*

Nuclear power plants can operate flexibly, even though they mostly operate in base-load mode. Nuclear power plants can be dispatched (i.e., turned on or off, or have output turned up or down) to meet varying electricity demand and manage system frequency if it makes economic sense to do so.

### *Clean*

Nuclear electricity is clean, emitting no carbon dioxide or other air pollutant emissions during operation. Nuclear power plants also have very low life-cycle greenhouse gas emissions during construction, operation, nuclear fuel cycle activities, and decommissioning.

Nuclear power lifecycle emissions are much lower than the emissions from combustion-based power plants, as shown in Figure 1. When nuclear power plants replace combustion-based power plants, emissions are reduced.

But when combustion-based power plants replace nuclear power plants, emissions are increased.

## Figure 1 - Lifecycle Greenhouse Gas Emissions

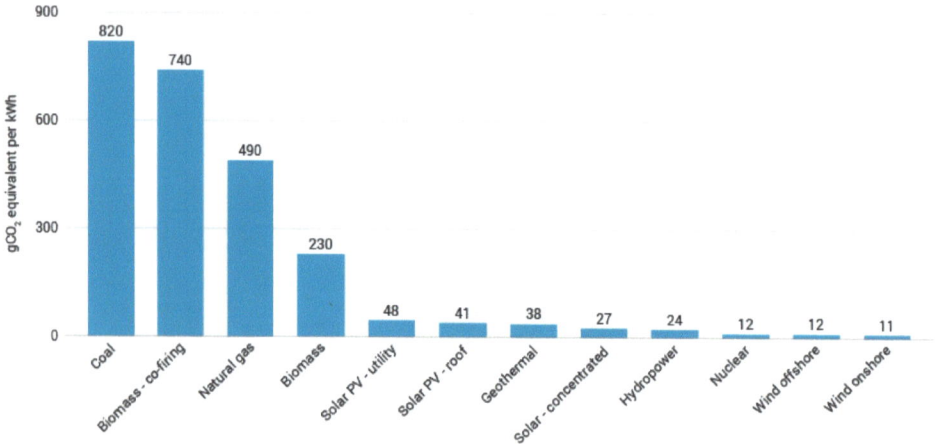

Source: *World Nuclear Association, How can nuclear combat climate change?* https://www.world-nuclear.org/nuclear-essentials/how-can-nuclear-combat-climate-change.aspx

### *Long-Lived*

Nuclear power plants can and do generate electricity for a very long time.

Nuclear power plants placed into commercial operation more than 40 years ago are still operating today. Many existing nuclear power plants have nuclear safety regulator approval to operate for 60 years. Some existing nuclear power plants may operate for 80 years or longer.

New nuclear power plants are designed and licensed to operate for 60 years and are expected to operate for 80 years or longer. Nuclear power plant life is two to three times longer than the life of combustion-based and renewable energy generation.

Comprehensive equipment maintenance and replacement programs ensure that nuclear power plants are in excellent condition, even after decades of full-power operation.

## Figure 2 - World Reactors by Age

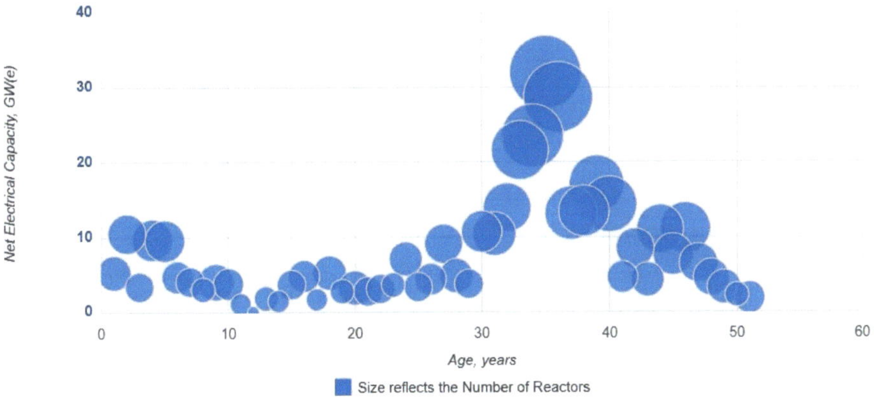

*Source: International Atomic Energy Agency Power Reactor Information System, October 2020 (https://pris.iaea.org/PRIS/WorldStatistics/OperationalByAge.aspx)*

### *Economic*

The cost of nuclear electricity is comparable to the cost of electricity from other generating options when considered over the 60+ year life of nuclear power plants.

Operational and investment economies of scale are an important aspect of nuclear power plant economics. Most nuclear power plants are large (i.e., 1,000 MWe or larger) to lower the cost of electricity per kilowatt-hour (kWh) by spreading fixed investment and generating costs over larger power output.

Nuclear electricity is very competitive when the full costs of other electricity generating options are included.[5]

The cost of electricity from combustion-based power plants should include the cost of carbon dioxide and other air pollution wastes released. The cost of electricity from wind and solar power plants should include the cost of system balancing and reliability reserves imposed by these intermittent generators. Electricity costs from other generation technologies should include decommissioning and disposal costs.

7

### *Scalable*

The transition to a zero-carbon electricity sector requires adding large amounts of new clean electricity generation capacity to replace combustion-based generation. Nuclear power can be built in significant amounts in a relatively short time (i.e., is highly scalable), as demonstrated in nuclear build programs in several countries.

The US and France both added about 5,000 MWe of new nuclear power plant capacity per year during their peak nuclear power build periods (i.e., 1971 to 1987 in the US, and 1979 to 1988 in France), as shown in Figure 3.

## Figure 3 - Nuclear Power Capacity

**Nuclear Power Capacity**

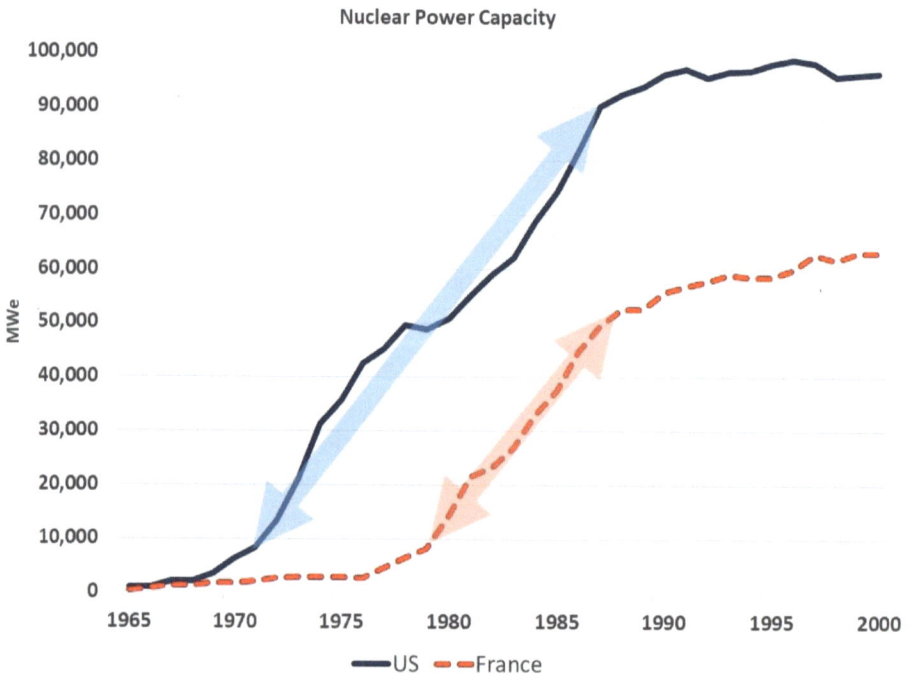

*Source: International Atomic Energy Agency Power Reactor Information System data, with analysis by the author.*

## *Compact*

Even the largest nuclear power plants are compact and require little land. Nuclear power land use is quite small when compared with the land required for wind and solar. Figure 4 shows a comparison of land use for the UK Hinkley Point C (HPC) project and a similar amount of wind and solar generation.

### Figure 4 - Nuclear Power Land Use Example

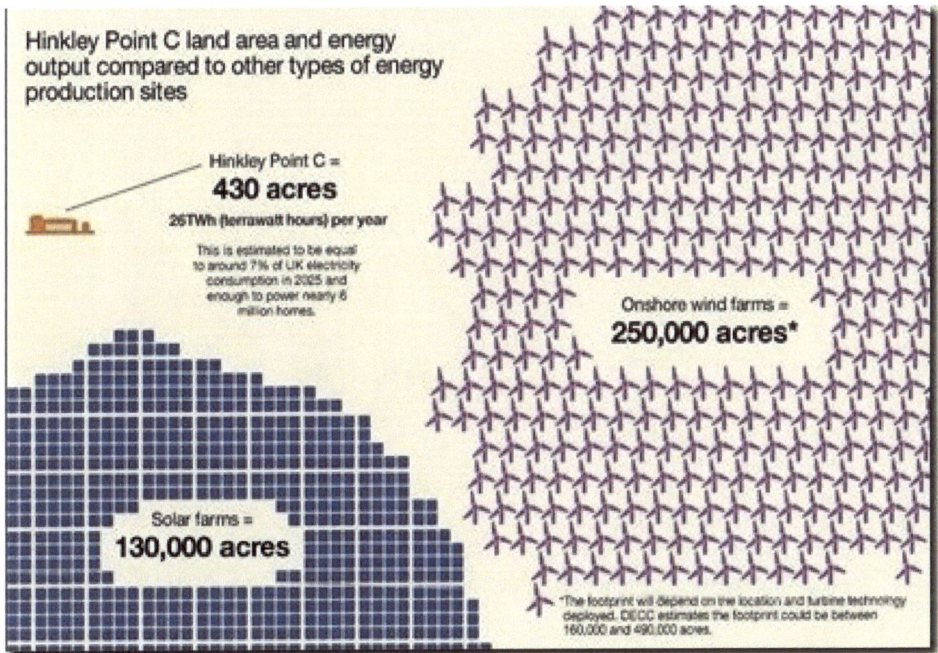

Hinkley Point C land area and energy output compared to other types of energy production sites

Hinkley Point C =
**430 acres**
26TWh (terrawatt hours) per year

This is estimated to be equal to around 7% of UK electricity consumption in 2025 and enough to power nearly 6 million homes.

Onshore wind farms =
**250,000 acres***

Solar farms =
**130,000 acres**

*The footprint will depend on the location and turbine technology deployed. DECC estimates the footprint could be between 160,000 and 490,000 acres.

*Source:* *http://neinuclearnotes.blogspot.com/2013/10/blighting-landscape-with-turbines.html*

## *Proven*

Hundreds of commercial nuclear power plants in multiple countries have millions of operating hours over more than a half-century. This extensive experience has led to better operating procedures, a deep nuclear safety culture, and important lessons for the next generation of nuclear power plants.

### *Safe*

Nuclear power is a very safe electricity generation technology, with fewer deaths per TWh of electricity generated than any other generation technology, even when conservatively high estimates of deaths from the few historical nuclear power accidents are included, as shown in Figure 5.

## Figure 5 - Deaths per TWh

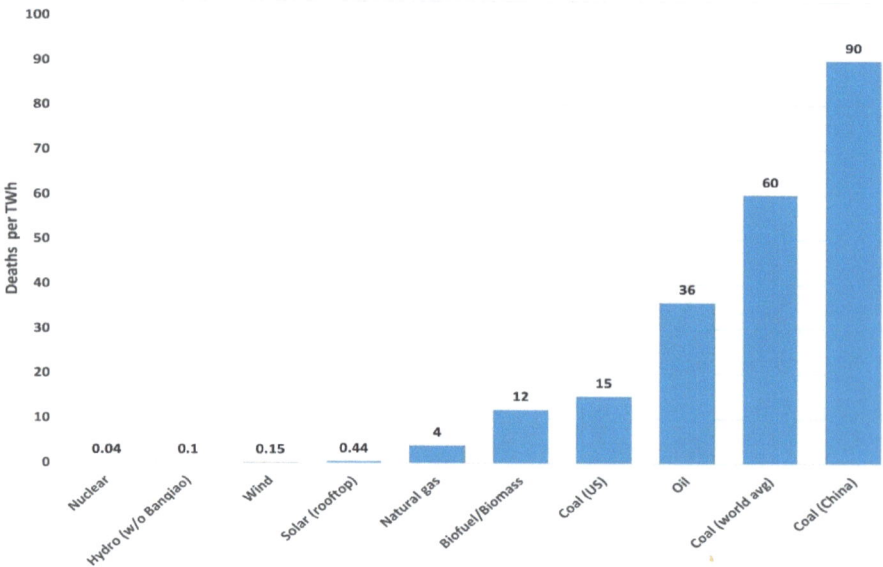

*Source: Data from Next Big Future, as presented in NECG Commentary #11 (https://nuclear-economics.com/11-nuclear-power-in-summer/).*

### *Skilled Jobs*

Nuclear power plants provide skilled and stable jobs.

Nuclear power plants provide more jobs than comparable combustion-based or renewable electricity generation plants. Nuclear power plants also require hundreds of short-term workers every 12-24 months during regular refueling and maintenance outages.

The positive economic impact of nuclear power jobs is most clearly seen when these jobs are lost due to a nuclear power plant closure.[6]

### *Electricity System Benefits*

Nuclear power plants provide a reliable source of generation to help maintain system reliability. In real time, nuclear power generators provide an important source of rotational inertia to manage electricity system frequency and voltage.[7]

# Insights

Nuclear power's positive attributes and benefits are well-established. Despite these positive attributes and benefits, the nuclear power industry is failing in countries where there is a market approach to the electricity industry.

# Market Failure

# NUCLEAR POWER

*"It takes up to 10 years to develop and build a new nuclear power plant that will then operate for 60 years or longer. Electricity markets and financial markets do not easily accommodate these long-term nuclear power plant assets."*

Edward Kee - *NECG Commentary #1 –*
*Long-Term Assets in a Short-Term World*[8]

This chapter provides background information on nuclear power, including basic terminology, nuclear power project phases, costs of nuclear electricity, operating modes, and the organization of nuclear power projects and the nuclear power industry.

# Terminology

The nuclear power industry uses terms that may not be familiar, and some of these are explained here.

### *Fission*

Nuclear power plants use energy from nuclear fission to generate electricity.

Nuclear fission happens with a neutron collides with a large uranium or plutonium atom, causing the large atom to split into several smaller atoms. Nuclear fission releases heat energy, radiation, and neutrons that can initiate other fission reactions. Under the right conditions, a self-sustaining nuclear fission chain reaction can be established. Nuclear reactors are designed to control a self-sustaining nuclear fission chain reaction to produce usable heat energy. Nuclear power plant heat energy is measured in MW thermal (MWth) and is limited by the nuclear safety regulator operating license, and the plant's electrical output, in MW electrical (MWe), is determined by the thermal efficiency of the power plant.

### *Nuclear Power*

A nuclear power plant generates electricity in several stages:

- Nuclear fission in the reactor core generates heat energy;
- Heat energy is removed from the reactor core by a reactor coolant;
- Heat energy is used to boil water to make steam; and
- The steam turns turbines that drive electricity generators.

A nuclear power plant is like a coal-fired steam power plant, but with the reactor core providing heat energy instead of a coal-fired boiler.

There are several types of nuclear power plants in commercial operation, with different reactor coolants, moderators, fuel types, and other features. The most common nuclear power plant designs are those using pressurized water reactor (PWR) and boiling water reactor (BWR) technology. These are referred to as light water reactor (LWR) designs, with both using normal water as a reactor coolant and moderator,

There are also different versions of these nuclear power plant technologies. For example, variants on the PWR nuclear power plant technology are available from suppliers in the US, Russia, France, South Korea, and China.

There are also new small and advanced reactor designs under development.[9] These new small and advanced reactor designs may achieve better project economics than conventional large nuclear power plant designs.

Any new nuclear power plant design faces challenges (e.g., large technology development cost, first-of-a-kind (FOAK) project cost, and unproven operational performance). These challenges are even higher if a new nuclear power plant design is developed by a private company in an electricity market.

Regardless of the nuclear reactor type, the electricity industry approach is an important factor in shaping project economics.

### *Reactors, Units, Plants, and Projects*

A nuclear power *reactor* contains the core and the nuclear fuel used to generates heat energy.

A nuclear power *unit* refers to a single reactor and turbine-generator set.

A nuclear power *plant* refers to a physical site where nuclear electricity is generated. A nuclear power plant may have one or more nuclear power units at the same site.

A nuclear power *project* refers to the overall process of developing and building a nuclear power plant.

### Nuclear Power Plants

This book refers to actual nuclear power plants. Information on these nuclear power plants can be found in the International Atomic Energy Agency (IAEA) Power Reactor Information System (PRIS) database (https://pris.iaea.org/pris/) and at the World Nuclear Association Reactor Database (https://www.world-nuclear.org/information-library/facts-and-figures/reactor-database.aspx).

### Light Water Reactors

LWR technology is used in most of the world's nuclear power plants, with 366 of 442 operating nuclear power reactors using LWR technology.[10]

PWR designs use pressurized light water as the moderator and primary reactor coolant to remove heat from the reactor core. Hot pressurized liquid (i.e., not steam) primary coolant is pumped through tubes inside a large heat exchanger, referred to as a steam generator, to generate steam, with this steam used to drive turbines. The primary high-pressure reactor coolant system is separate from the secondary steam system, adding a barrier between the core and the environment. PWR technology is used in 302 of the 442 nuclear power reactors in operation.[11]

BWR designs also use light water as a moderator and coolant to remove heat from the reactor core. Unlike a PWR, BWR reactor primary coolant boils to allow steam to be generated directly in the core. This steam is used to drive turbines. The BWR design avoids the primary coolant loop and steam generators in the PWR design but has one less barrier between the core and the environment. 64 of the 442 nuclear power reactors in operation use BWR technology.[12]

### Other reactor designs

There are other reactor designs in operation in addition to LWR technology. Pressurized Heavy Water Reactor (PHWR)[13] power plants are operating in Canada, India, Romania, South Korea, Argentina, Pakistan, and

China, with 48 of the 442 nuclear power reactors in operation using PHWR technology.[14]

There are also other types of reactors in operation, including gas-cooled reactors (e.g., the UK AGR designs).

### *Nuclear Technology Evolution*

The evolution of nuclear power technology has been slower than some other technologies. This slow pace of change is due to nuclear power plants' long operating life and the relatively recent discovery of nuclear fission. As shown in Figure 2, many operating nuclear power plants have been in operation for more than 30 years.

Classifying nuclear power plant technology by vintage, technology approach, and size provides a useful framework.[15] Only a few generations of nuclear power plants have been built and placed into operation, with new advanced and Small Modular Reactors (SMRs) under development.[16] This framework is shown in Figure 6 and discussed below.

### Figure 6 - Nuclear Power Technology Generations

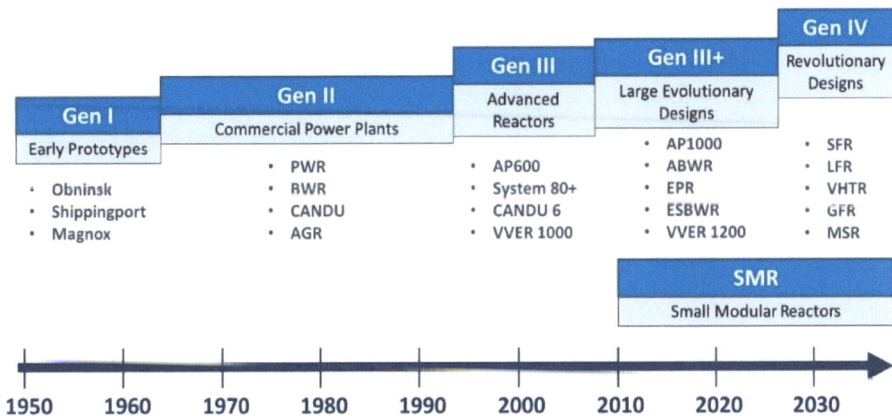

### Gen I

The first generation of nuclear power plants were early prototypes of civilian power reactors built in the 1950s and 1960s, referred to as Generation I (Gen I). Gen I nuclear power plants demonstrated the technical and commercial feasibility of using nuclear fission to generate electricity. All Gen I nuclear power plants are closed.

Gen I nuclear power plants used a wide range of reactor and power plant designs. Gen I nuclear power plants were small, about the same size as modern SMR nuclear power plants. However, Gen I nuclear power plants did not have the advanced features used in today's SMR technologies.

### Gen II

The second generation of commercial nuclear power plants, referred to as Generation II (Gen II), was developed starting in the 1960s based on the technology concepts proven in Gen I nuclear power plants. Gen II nuclear power plants had more advanced nuclear safety systems, were designed for civilian power use, and were larger (i.e., to capture scale economies).

Gen II nuclear power plants typically started operation with a 40-year operating license from a nuclear safety regulator. In the US and other countries, some Gen II nuclear power plants have received approval to operate for an additional 20 years (i.e., 60 years of operation). Gen II nuclear power plants are expected to operate even longer than 60 years, and the US NRC has developed a process to review applications for Gen II nuclear power plants to operate for an additional 20 years (i.e., 80 total years of operation).

Decades of operational experience with Gen II nuclear power plants provides the nuclear power industry with learning on the operation, safety, and maintenance of nuclear power plants.

### Gen III

The third generation of nuclear power plants, referred to as Generation III (Gen III), incorporates the extensive learning from decades of Gen II nuclear power plant operation.

Gen III nuclear power plant designs include additional safety features, larger generating capacity (i.e., to capture economies of scale), longer operating life, and more extensive use of advanced construction methods (e.g., top-down modular construction) compared to Gen II.

Gen III nuclear power plants have reactor safety margins about ten times higher than Gen II nuclear power plant designs. Gen III nuclear power plants are designed for a 60-year operating life, and are expected to operate for 100 years or longer.

The first Gen III units are the Japanese Advanced Boiling Water Reactor (ABWR) projects placed into commercial operation in the late 1990s. The Chinese nuclear power fleet includes several Chinese Gen III reactor designs and imported Gen III reactor designs from the US, France, and Russia. South Korea developed the APR-1400 design, with units built in South Korea and the UAE.

Some of these Gen III units are referred to as Gen III+. While the industry does not have a clear definition, Gen III+ reactors are typically GEN III designs with more extensive safety systems (e.g., passive safety) and other features.

China and Russia are actively building large nuclear power plants using Gen III technology, with a few Gen III nuclear power projects under construction in Finland, France, the US, the UK, the UAE, and other countries.

### SMRs

The larger capacity of Gen II and III nuclear power plants was intended to capture economies of scale in construction and operation. However, these larger nuclear power plants have high total capital cost and may be more likely to have project cost overruns and schedule delays.

SMR designs are intended to address the high total capital cost and project development issues seen in some large nuclear power plants. The SMR designs are under development have some common themes.

SMR nuclear power plants are smaller than large nuclear power plants. Smaller size reduces the initial total capital investment for an SMR project compared to Gen III projects, and the lower total cost should make SMR projects easier to fund. The smaller size also allows SMR projects to fit into smaller electricity systems and countries where large nuclear power plants would not be a good fit.

The loss of scale economies may increase SMR costs per MWe of output. SMR concepts aim to offset this potential increase in capital costs per MWe by factory production of modules, modular construction, fewer safety requirements, learning across multiple units, and other factors.

Smaller SMR size facilitates a shift to building reactors in an off-site factory and transporting them to the power plant site. Factory production of SMR modules could lower costs, increase quality, and shorten time-to-build. The smaller size of SMRs also facilitates a modular construction approach that may reduce capital cost risk and shorten construction schedules compared to the on-site construction used in large nuclear power plants.

SMR designs include innovative reactor safety features that remove the requirement for some safety equipment (e.g., emergency generators, safety injection pumps, and emergency cooling systems) that increases the cost of large nuclear power plant designs. SMR designs may lower capital and operating costs by relying on safety by design rather than safety by added systems.

Multiple SMR nuclear power plants will be needed to replace a single large nuclear power plant, so more SMR nuclear power plants would be built to meet the demand for nuclear electricity. Building multiple SMR nuclear power plants that use identical factory-built reactors and modules should lower cost-to-build and time-to-build for later units due to learning.

SMR designs are mostly variants of existing Gen III technology, including integral PWR and smaller BWR designs. Some SMRs use advanced reactor concepts that are considered Gen IV. SMRs also include microreactors that are smaller than 20 MWe.[17]

SMR nuclear power plants are now in the licensing and development stage. Russia has completed its first floating SMR (i.e., the KLT-40 Academician Lomonosov power plant), and China is building prototypes of multiple SMR designs.

If the promise of SMR designs to deliver lower costs can be demonstrated, there is a potential that these smaller reactor designs will gain a significant share of the nuclear power market. Demonstrating these new reactor designs' economics will require building and operating FOAK SMR nuclear power plant projects to get real information on these new SMR designs' economic performance.

Even if SMR designs can match, or improve on, large reactor economics, some fundamental economic features – large initial capital cost, substantial time to develop and build, long operating lives, and zero marginal cost – will remain the same. It is highly unlikely that SMR designs can overcome the issues presented by a market approach to electricity and nuclear power.

### Gen IV

Research into advanced reactor designs, referred to as Generation IV (Gen IV), started at the beginning of the nuclear power industry. Some Gen I technologies used reactor concepts that are now considered Gen IV technologies.

Gen IV reactor design concepts include the Sodium-cooled Fast Reactor (SFR), Very High Temperature Reactor (VHTR), Super Critical Water Reactor (SCWR), Lead-cooled Fast Reactor (LFR), Gas-cooled Fast Reactor (GFR), Molten Salt Reactor (MSR), and other concepts.

Gen IV reactor designs typically have higher temperature heat energy, increased resistance to accidents, a closed fuel cycle, and enhanced proliferation resistance.

Russia and China have several Gen IV nuclear power plants in operation.

Gen IV reactor designs, like SMR designs, offer a promise that some of the issues with large conventional reactors (e.g., safety, cost, and fuel cycle) can be overcome.

### Regulation

In the nuclear power industry, there are multiple types of regulation.

### *Nuclear Safety Regulation*

A national nuclear safety regulator like the US Nuclear Regulatory Commission (NRC) has oversight of nuclear power plant and reactor designs, nuclear power plant operation, and radioactive materials.

The typical objective of a nuclear safety regulator is to ensure public health and safety.[18] Nuclear safety regulators typically license and regulate:

- Commercial reactors for generating electric power;

- Research and test reactors;

- Use of nuclear materials in facilities that produce nuclear fuel;

- Use of nuclear materials in medical, industrial, and academic applications;

- Transportation, storage, and disposal of nuclear materials and radioactive waste; and

- Decommissioning of nuclear facilities.

Each country has its own national nuclear safety regulator and its own approach to nuclear safety regulation. In Japan, local political jurisdictions have an informal but powerful role in deciding on nuclear power plants' continued operation. In contrast, the US NRC has sole authority over nuclear safety issues.

The independence of nuclear safety regulators is important.

### *Economic Regulation*

The nuclear power industry operates in the electricity industry and may have oversight from an economic regulator.

Electricity industry economic regulators oversee investment decisions for nuclear power and other new power plant investments, determine how power plant investments are recovered, set rates (i.e., prices) for electricity, and have other responsibilities.

In most countries, the economic regulator is separate from the nuclear safety regulator. Economic regulators may be independent (e.g., US state utility commissions) or may be a part of a country's government (e.g., Ministry of Energy).

### *Other Regulation*

Nuclear power plants and nuclear industrial companies are also subject to other regulators, including those that oversee occupational health and safety, environmental protection, and securities and financial issues.

Other issues like national tax laws, local property tax assessments, and local emergency notification/response requirements may impact nuclear project profitability and operation.

Regulators that oversee wholesale electricity transactions and electricity markets may be very important for nuclear power plants that operate in those markets.

## Nuclear Project Phases

Nuclear power project phases, shown in Figure 7, cover a total period of 100 years or longer.

### Figure 7 - Nuclear Project Phases

Development & Evaluation | Construction | Commercial Operation | Decommissioning

### *Evaluation & Development*

The Evaluation and Development Phase may take several years. In some instances, projects have spent decades in this phase, and some do not make it past this stage.

This phase begins with a proposal to build a new nuclear plant and ends with a Financial Investment Decision, where sponsors and lenders decide to fund the project and commit to construction. This phase may also end when project sponsors decide to postpone the project or to cancel it.

This phase usually includes initial evaluation activity to explore the potential for a new nuclear power project that requires limited investment, followed by more substantial development activity that requires a potentially large investment.

Project development starts when project sponsors commit to funding feasibility studies, applying for licenses, negotiating contracts to buy and build the nuclear power plant, arranging the plant's financing, and other activities. Project costs incurred before a project Financial Investment Decision is made (or before the project is canceled) may be significant.

For example, obtaining a Combined Construction and Operation License (COL) from the US Nuclear Regulatory Commission (NRC) may cost more than US$1 billion.

Regulated investor-owned utilities can usually recover the costs of developing a credible nuclear power option (i.e., including, in the US, some or all the cost of obtaining an NRC COL license) from regulated utility customers, and government utilities recover project development costs from taxpayers. However, merchant nuclear power plant developers will only recover development costs after a nuclear power plant is built and placed into commercial operation.

The time spent on design, engineering, planning, and other similar activities in the Evaluation and Development Phase for a nuclear power plant is important. This design and engineering activity will ensure that sound analyses support the decision to fund and construct the nuclear power plant and reduce the potential for cost overruns and delays during construction.

During this phase, a project financial model will be developed to estimate cash flows over the nuclear power project's life. This financial model will also be used to evaluate scenarios related to capital cost, timing, revenue, and other factors that influence project cash flow. This financial model is the primary tool to communicate with potential project lenders, investors, power off-take customers, economic regulators, and other stakeholders. A project financial model will provide much of the information needed to support a Financial Investment Decision.

After a Financial Investment Decision to proceed, construction starts.

### *Construction*

The Construction Phase takes five years or longer. Nuclear power plant construction includes multiple activities, including site preparation, civil engineering, fabrication of major nuclear power plant components, on-site construction and assembly, fuel loading and initial criticality testing, and initial power testing.

A nuclear power project involves different construction activities, only some of which require approval from the nuclear safety regulator. The start of nuclear construction is when work begins on items subject to nuclear safety regulator oversight, with the typical first activity being the pouring of so-called safety-related concrete for the reactor basement or foundation. Significant activity and expenditure may occur before nuclear construction starts.

The primary concern in this phase is the cost and time required to complete the nuclear power plant. Cost overruns and schedule delays are common in nuclear power and other mega-projects due to large size, complex systems, reactor safety regulator oversight, and many parties and activities. Schedule delays increase project costs because of higher interest costs during construction and the cost of keeping construction crews mobilized at the site during delays.

In some projects, cost overruns and schedule delays cause the project to be abandoned before completion but after a substantial investment has been made.

Completion risk is the risk of cost or time overruns and project abandonment. With nuclear power projects having total budgets in the billions of dollars, completion risk is a significant issue.

If the nuclear power project's target commercial operation date is delayed, there may be financial consequences in addition to capital cost increases. The nuclear power plant's ultimate owners may have to buy replacement power from other sources if the delayed nuclear power plant capacity is a key part of their generation expansion plan. Depending on the nuclear power project's commercial arrangements, the nuclear power plant vendor may be required to pay replacement power costs or liquidated damages for delays. Delays in completing a merchant nuclear power plant will mean delayed revenue and lower returns on investment for the nuclear power plant owner.

The Construction Phase ends when the nuclear power plant is completed and placed into commercial operation (i.e., the plant's Commercial Operation Date).

### *Commercial Operation*

The Commercial Operation phase lasts 60 or more years, during which the nuclear power plant generates electricity that is delivered to the bulk power grid. This power is sold, to power contract counterparties, into an electricity market, or to the end-use customers of a regulated vertically-integrated utility.

During this phase, the primary concern is whether revenue from the sale of power will cover generating costs and provide a return on investment, referred to as revenue risk. A nuclear power plant may be less profitable than expected because revenue is lower, generating costs are higher, output or capacity factor is lower, there is a prolonged outage, unplanned plant modifications (i.e., new safety features) are required, or other reasons.

As outlined below, electricity markets in the US and other countries have uncertain prices, so that revenue over the 60-year life of a nuclear power plant is uncertain. This uncertainty applies directly to a merchant nuclear plant that sells power into an electricity market and may indirectly influence a regulated or government nuclear power plant's value.

The Commercial Operation phase ends when the nuclear power plant is shut down, the operating license is terminated, and the decommissioning plan is implemented.

### Decommissioning

The Decommissioning Phase can last for decades. Decommissioning involves the dismantlement and removal of the nuclear power plant and site remediation/restoration. National requirements determine the approach to decommissioning. Depending on the decommissioning approach, it might be 60 years or more after a nuclear power plant closes for the plant to be entirely decommissioned.

Nuclear power plants are typically required to accumulate money during the commercial operation phase to fund decommissioning. A nuclear power plant will also have to fund the disposition of spent nuclear fuel (SNF). Contributions to decommissioning funds and SNF disposition funds are included in the cost of nuclear electricity during operation. Nuclear power plants typically have more robust decommissioning requirements than other power generation technologies, with nuclear power decommissioning fund balances of hundreds of millions of dollars.

The primary concern in this phase is that decommissioning and SNF disposition funds (or the credit-worthiness of the party responsible for costs of decommissioning) will not cover the costs of decommissioning and SNF disposition. Designing funds, assigning responsibility for costs, and deciding how any shortfalls will be addressed are important factors.

# Nuclear Power Costs

### Capital Cost

Nuclear power plants are capital-intensive projects with substantial up-front capital costs. After completion, these nuclear power plants deliver electricity with low and stable generating costs for 60 years or longer.

Nuclear power plant capital costs have historically been higher than estimated. An important issue for any nuclear power project is understanding and managing capital costs.

Nuclear power plant cost overruns may be caused by several factors, including optimistic or unrealistic capital cost estimates, inadequate up-front project design and engineering, and modifications during construction. Nuclear power plant projects that use FOAK reactor designs and those in countries without nuclear power experience are more likely to experience cost overruns. Nuclear power plant cost overruns have led to bankruptcies (e.g., Westinghouse, which declared bankruptcy in 2017), nuclear project abandonment after construction start (e.g., the V.C. Summer project in 2017), and substantial financial losses.[19]

### *Generating Cost*

Nuclear power plants incur costs to generate electricity, including the cost of nuclear fuel, operating and maintenance (O&M) activity, and ongoing capital expenditures.

### *Nuclear fuel cost*

Nuclear fuel is a complex manufactured product, unlike the bulk commodity fuels (e.g., coal, petroleum, natural gas) burned in combustion-based generation technologies.

LWR nuclear fuel is manufactured by mining and refining uranium, making enriched uranium fuel pellets placed into fuel tubes, and joining fuel tubes together into fuel assemblies. A fuel assembly is loaded into a reactor core, where it remains for about six years before it is replaced with a new fuel assembly.

The energy density of uranium is much greater than combustion fuels, so nuclear power plants only need to be refueled every 18 to 24 months. About a third of the fuel is replaced during a refueling and maintenance outage that takes about a month.

The LWR batch refueling approach means that nuclear fuel costs are incurred months or years before fuel is loaded into a reactor and that nuclear fuel costs do not change with short-term changes in plant output.

### O&M cost

Nuclear power plant O&M costs are mostly personnel costs, including nuclear power plant operators, maintenance staff, site security, training, engineering, information technology (IT), quality assurance (QA), office support staff, and other staff. During regular refueling/maintenance outages, many temporary contract workers are used.

O&M costs are fixed and are incurred if the nuclear power plant is operational (i.e., has an operating license), whether it is generating power or not. O&M costs per MWh are lower for a nuclear power plant that operates more (i.e., has a high capacity factor) because the fixed O&M costs are spread across more MWh of output.

Nuclear power plant O&M costs have economies of scale that lead to lower O&M costs per MWh for larger, multi-unit plants. A small single-unit nuclear power plant may require similar staffing as a larger nuclear power plant, resulting in higher O&M costs per MWh for the small nuclear power plant.

### Capital expenditures

In addition to normal maintenance, nuclear power plants undertake substantial preventive maintenance and component replacement. The cost of replacing some components may qualify as a capital expenditure under accounting rules, and these capital expenditures can be depreciated. Like O&M costs, capital expenditure costs are fixed and are not linked to the nuclear power plant's short-term electricity generation output.

### Fixed and Marginal Costs

Unlike combustion-based power plants, where fuel and other generating costs are linked to power plant output, nuclear power plant generating costs are fixed and are not linked to the plant's power level. Fixed generating cost means that nuclear power plants have a short-run marginal cost (SRMC) of zero.[20]

However, the nuclear power SRMC of zero may change due to some administrative payments or charges. For example, the zero-emission credit (ZEC) payments to nuclear power plants in some US states and proposed federal production tax credit (PTC) incentives for new nuclear power projects are based on nuclear power plant output. These ZEC and PTC schemes result in a negative contribution to nuclear power plant SRMC (i.e., revenue is lower when output is lower).

Another example is a nuclear waste fee collected on each kWh of nuclear power plant output.[21] This waste fee approach results in a positive contribution to nuclear power plant SRMC (i.e., waste fee costs are lower when output is lower).

### *Economies of Scale*

The nuclear power industry has developed large reactors and large multi-reactor power plant sites to lower nuclear power plant capital and generating cost.

Multi-unit nuclear power plants can lower the cost per MWh of site security, administration, support, cooling water infrastructure, and other items by sharing these costs across multiple units on the same site. Multi-unit nuclear power plants can shut down one unit for refueling and maintenance while generating power with the other units on the site. A multi-unit nuclear power plant may also lower the costs of connecting the plant to the grid for similar reasons (i.e., one large transmission line rather than several transmission lines).

There has been increased interest in small modular reactors (SMRs) and new advanced reactor designs in the last decade. These new small and advanced reactor designs promise lower capital costs and faster time to build but have not yet demonstrated that they have the same or lower costs than large reactors.

# Nuclear Power Operations

*"Some industry observers conclude that nuclear power plants cannot operate flexibly because most of them operate in base-load mode (i.e., not as flexible generators). This is not correct. Nuclear power plants can operate flexibly."*

Edward Kee - *NECG Commentary #3 – Nuclear Base Load*[22]

Nuclear power plants are almost exclusively operated to generate electricity that is delivered to the bulk power system.

### *Operating Mode*

Vertically-integrated electric utilities own and operate power plants to meet the demand of the customers they serve. Operating low-SRMC generating options (e.g., nuclear and hydroelectric power plants) instead of high-SRMC options (e.g., combustion-based power plants) lowers total system cost. This economic system dispatch approach is a fundamental part of utility operations.

Electricity markets are designed to achieve similar economic system dispatch, with the lowest-marginal-cost generators, including nuclear power, operated before higher-marginal cost generating options.

System dispatch is complicated by electricity system demand that varies over the day, the week, and the year. The minimum annual system demand is known as base-load demand.

Economic system dispatch, whether in a vertically-integrated traditional utility or an electricity market, results in nuclear power plants being dispatched first to meet base-load demand whenever these nuclear power plants are available because of nuclear power's SRMC of zero.[23]

### *Flexible Operation*

Decades of experience operating nuclear power plants in base-load mode have led operators to adopt practices that maximize performance and lower generating costs in base-load operation.

Some industry observers incorrectly conclude that nuclear power plants can only operate in base-load mode and cannot operate as flexible generators.

Nuclear power plants can operate flexibly.[24] However, a nuclear power plant in flexible operation mode has lower electricity output, lower revenue and profits in electricity markets, higher generating costs, and increased risk of unplanned outages than operating the same nuclear power plant in base-load mode.

There are examples of nuclear power plants operating flexibly.

The Bruce Power plant in Ontario provides fast-response output change capability to help the market operator manage wind energy output changes. Bruce Power operates flexibly by bypassing steam turbines to send steam directly to condensers. Bruce Power is compensated for the output it would have produced without flexible operation and is paid to undertake plant modifications to enhance flexible operation capability.[25]

France operates its nuclear power fleet flexibly to follow load and manage system frequency. Flexible operation is needed because nuclear power provides about 75% of total electricity in France.[26] French nuclear power plant flexible operation is enhanced by control rod technology and a coordinated fleet dispatch approach. Flexible nuclear power plant operation is supported by Electricité de France (EDF) ownership of the entire electricity system and full recovery of nuclear power plant costs, regardless of nuclear plant output.

The US Columbia Generating Station nuclear power plant operates flexibly to help manage the US Pacific Northwest's extensive hydroelectric power system.[27] Columbia output is changed in response to requests from the regional grid system operator, the Bonneville Power Authority (BPA).

Columbia's flexible operation arrangements are facilitated by cost-based power contracts between BPA and Columbia's public power owners.

Exelon operates selected nuclear power plants in western Illinois at lower output levels when negative electricity market prices are expected. Lowering nuclear power plant output when electricity market prices are negative improves nuclear power plant profits by lowering payments to the market operator for power deliveries during negative price periods.

In 2020, EDF Energy's Sizewell B nuclear power plant in the UK was operated for four months at half its normal output to help the UK grid manage low demand due to COVID-19. National Grid compensated EDF Energy for this action.[28]

### Long-Term Flexibility

The discussion of nuclear power plant flexible operation has, so far, focused on short-term (i.e., hourly, daily, or seasonal) variations in output. There are also situations where long-term flexibility (e.g., a nuclear power plant is closed for years and then restarted) has value.

Nuclear power plant generating costs may be higher than current and near-term projections of electricity market prices, resulting in current and projected financial losses for a merchant nuclear power plant. If low electricity market prices are expected to last for several years, a merchant nuclear power plant owner may decide that the best financial strategy is to close the nuclear power plant.

There are several options for a merchant nuclear power plant facing financial losses.

One option is that the nuclear power plant continues operation with financial losses, with the nuclear power plant potentially having value if future electricity market prices increase. The nuclear power plant is a real option, with the cost of maintaining the real option being near-term financial losses.

Another option is to close the nuclear power plant to stop financial losses. In the US, this means early and permanent closure, so that there is no option to restart the plant later when market conditions improve. So far, several US merchant nuclear power plants (e.g., Kewaunee and Vermont Yankee) closed early and permanently because of current and expected financial losses in electricity markets.

Another option, not available in the US, is to close the nuclear power plant to restart it later. This mothball option would allow a nuclear power plant to close and substantially reduce costs during periods when electricity prices are low but allow the plant to be restarted when market conditions improve.[29] This mothball option would increase the real option value of a merchant nuclear power plant, but there is no existing process for this mothball strategy in the US.

A nuclear power mothball option is available in Canada. In 1997, four units at the Pickering nuclear power plant were mothballed due to overcapacity in Ontario, with two of these units returned to service in 2003 and 2005. Between 1995 and 1998, four reactors at the Bruce nuclear power plant were mothballed, with two returned to service in 2003 and 2004, and the other two returned to service in 2012. The mothball option kept these plants available for a later restart and full commercial operation and increased their value.

### Other Products

The primary revenue source for nuclear power plants is selling wholesale electricity. However, additional revenue for these nuclear power markets may come from side markets (i.e., markets that operate outside the wholesale electricity spot market) or non-electricity products. These side markets and additional products may provide additional revenue for a nuclear power plant.

A common side market is a capacity market, where payments are based on plant capacity rather than electricity output. Capacity markets may require a power plant to remain in commercial operation for several years. Capacity markets provide additional revenue but may limit a nuclear power plant owner's options to close the power plant.

Another side market is for flexible fast-response generation. A nuclear power plant might provide fast response generation needed by a grid operator to respond to fluctuations in system demand or intermittent generator output. Providing fast-response generation from a nuclear power plant will mean less revenue from electricity sales, and this product's compensation must reflect these losses.

Nuclear power plants can provide heat energy for various applications that could provide additional revenue. Heat energy may be used for low-temperature applications (e.g., district heating) or higher temperature applications (e.g., industrial processes). Removing heat energy may require additional equipment and capital expenditures and may mean that a nuclear power plant generates less electricity.

Additional nuclear power plant revenue might come from co-locating energy storage, hydrogen production, or desalination facilities on the nuclear power plant site. Other additional revenue options may include electrically-driven reverse osmosis (RO) desalination using nuclear power plant electrical output but located at a different site (e.g., where water is needed).

# Industry Organization and Business Models

The nuclear power industry has a mix of private and government industrial companies. Some of these nuclear industrial companies focus on one aspect of the industry (e.g., reactors, nuclear fuel, or construction), while other companies have integrated product offerings.

The companies that invest in, own, and operate nuclear power plants include regulated utilities, government-owned utilities, and new merchant nuclear entities.

### *Nuclear Power Industrial Sector*

Nuclear industrial company mergers and acquisitions have led to fewer private companies that design and build nuclear power plants over several decades. At the same time, new state-owned nuclear industrial companies now compete in the world market.

State-owned nuclear industrial companies have a large share of their home country's nuclear power market. Assured sales into the domestic nuclear power plant market allow a state-owned nuclear industrial company to develop and license new nuclear power plant designs, build nuclear power plants using these designs, and develop a proven nuclear power supply chain. This domestic nuclear power activity provides a strong platform for the state-owned nuclear vendor to compete in the world nuclear power market. State-owned nuclear industrial companies may have objectives other than profits from selling nuclear power plants, including importing nuclear power jobs, locking in long-term nuclear fuel and services sales, and enhancing national geopolitical influence.

In the last decade, new companies developing SMR and advanced reactor designs have also entered the nuclear power industry.

### *Nuclear Power Plant Owners and Operators*

Consolidation has also taken place in owners and operators of nuclear power plants, with a trend toward companies that own and operate nuclear power plant fleets. A nuclear power plant fleet owner can maintain and operate the nuclear power plants in its fleet with lower costs and better performance than a company that owns and operates a single nuclear power plant.

The traditional vertically-integrated utility approach to building and owning nuclear power plants was used in all operating commercial nuclear power plants in the world today. However, new approaches to developing, building, and owning nuclear power plants are emerging as the electricity industry has changed.

### *Traditional Approach*

Traditional nuclear power plant ownership, in the traditional approach, has a vertically-integrated electric utility that owns and operates a portfolio of non-nuclear and nuclear power plants to generate electricity that is delivered and sold to its retail customers.

One version of the traditional approach is where a government utility builds, owns, and operates nuclear power plants. France, the pre-reform UK, Russia, China, and other countries have government nuclear power sectors. The government invests in one or more nuclear power plants and recovers the investment from electricity sales to utility customers and, as needed, from tax revenue. The government also acts as an economic regulator, overseeing investment decisions and setting electricity sales rates. When the government owns both the electricity and nuclear power industrial sectors, the entire nuclear power value chain is under government control. The government can make strategy and investment decisions that reflect the full set of nuclear power costs and benefits, not just commodity electricity market prices.

Another version of the traditional approach is the US, Japan, and other countries' regulated investor-owned utility approach. A regulated utility develops, owns, and operates nuclear power plants subject to economic oversight by a utility economic regulator. Electricity economic regulators oversee regulated utility strategy and investment decisions that reflect the full set of nuclear power costs and benefits, not just commodity electricity market prices.

In this approach, electricity economic regulators also protect ratepayers. A regulated utility's shareholders may face potential financial impacts when a nuclear power project is over budget or behind schedule, when the economic regulator requires utility shareholders, not ratepayers, to pay for a part of the nuclear power project (i.e., a disallowance).[30]

Traditional nuclear power plant investments are based on the high degree of revenue certainty that the traditional approach provides for government and regulated electric utilities. However, the potential for regulated utility nuclear power investment disallowances makes government investments a more certain way forward.

### New Approaches

In recent decades, new nuclear power plant business models have emerged. These new business models reflect changes in the electricity industry and draw on experience with non-nuclear independent power producer (IPP) projects.

An IPP is a stand-alone company that develops, owns, and operates a power plant to sell wholesale electricity. IPP projects may also be called merchant or Build Own and Operate (BOO) projects. IPP projects sell electricity to generate revenue to cover generating costs, debt service, and returns to investors. IPP project risk is managed by contracts, including fixed-price contracts to build the power plant, long-term power contracts to sell electricity, contracts to operate and maintain the power plant, and fuel supply contracts. This set of contracts allows the IPP to be financed based only on project profits without recourse to project equity investors.

The IPP approach, including non-recourse project financing, has not been used in any nuclear power project, reflecting the higher risk in nuclear power projects.

Some existing nuclear power plants built under the traditional electricity industry approach have been divested or privatized, converting them into merchant nuclear plants operating like non-nuclear IPP projects. US merchant nuclear generators are examples of this.

Some new nuclear power plant projects are being developed using the IPP business model. These nuclear IPP projects involve the assumption of substantial risk by investors, a big difference from the stand-alone non-recourse non-nuclear IPP model. So far, new nuclear IPP projects have only been developed by reactor vendors.

Nuclear power plant vendors may be investors in a nuclear power IPP project using their reactor designs. By developing its own nuclear IPP project, the reactor vendor can avoid a competitive bidding process and the risk of losses associated with a fixed price contract that might be needed to make a sale. Instead, the reactor vendor has a certain sale and the opportunity to earn profits over the nuclear power plant project's life. The IPP model also provides the vendor with more control over the nuclear power project. This vendor-led nuclear power IPP model may be especially useful when the reactor vendor builds the first units of a new nuclear power plant design.

The only vendor-led nuclear power IPP projects under construction have state-owned nuclear industrial companies as owners. Governments may be the only entities that can make the high-risk, large-scale, and long-term financial commitment required for a new nuclear IPP.

The nuclear power IPP model may also require the project developer to be a nuclear power plant owner and operator. It will be difficult for a shareholder-owned nuclear industrial company (e.g., Toshiba, Hitachi, and

Mitsubishi) to transform itself into a nuclear power plant developer, builder, owner, and operator to develop a nuclear power IPP project.

# Nuclear Power Project Issues

Nuclear project issues include completion and revenue risk. The industry has developed approaches that help manage these risks, including vertical integration. Other aspects of nuclear power include transaction costs, nuclear fleet approaches, national nuclear power companies, and national nuclear champions.

### *Completion Risk*

One or more of the parties involved in a new nuclear project must take the financial consequences of completion risk (i.e., the project costs more than expected, takes longer to build than expected, or is abandoned after construction begins).

A nuclear power plant buyer might take completion risk if this risk can be transferred to customers (e.g., government and regulated investor-owned utilities) or to taxpayers (e.g., government utilities).

Nuclear power vendors might take completion risk by contracting to sell a nuclear power plant at a fixed price. Vendors may also take completion risk by developing and owning a nuclear power IPP project using their reactor design.

Truly independent nuclear power IPP project developers operating in a deregulated electricity market with little long-term revenue certainty are unlikely to take completion risk.

### *FOAK Risk*

Developing, licensing, and building a FOAK reactor design presents a higher completion risk than projects using proven reactor designs.

One way to limit FOAK risk is to use a new reactor design with incremental changes to a licensed and operational reactor design. FOAK risk may be higher for new and innovative reactor designs.

FOAK risk also applies to nuclear power plants built by a company with little recent experience with nuclear power plant construction and nuclear power plants built in countries where nuclear safety regulators and other government entities overseeing nuclear power projects have little recent experience.

A vendor might accept completion risk for a FOAK nuclear power plant project to get the first unit of a new design built.

### Nuclear EPC Contracts

Nuclear power plants are purchased using an Engineering, Procurement, and Construction (EPC) contract with a nuclear power plant vendor (or a consortium of vendors). An EPC contractor develops the nuclear power project from commencement to completion based on the buyer's requirements and specifications. An EPC contract that puts full responsibility on the vendor is sometimes referred to as a turnkey contract.

EPC contracts may have different compensation types, including fixed-price or lump sum contracts and reimbursement or cost-plus-fee contracts. The buyer's price risk is lower under a fixed price or lump sum contract and is higher under a reimbursement or cost-plus-fee contract.

### Lump-Sum Turnkey Contracts

A lump-sum turnkey (LSTK) contract is an approach that places all responsibility for project design, engineering, and delivery on the contractor for a fixed lump-sum amount. In theory, this places all project completion risk on the contractor and none on the buyer. However, if an LSTK contractor defaults, the buyer may have to pay more for the same contractor or a different contractor to complete the project.

Nuclear power plant vendors may enter into LSTK contracts for multiple reasons.

Early nuclear power LSTK contracts were used to sell the first nuclear power plants by selling a nuclear power plant with an LSTK contract price comparable to a coal-fired power plant price.[31]  An early example of this approach was in the US Oyster Creek nuclear power plant.[32]

A nuclear power plant vendor may sell a new reactor design using an LSTK contract to create an operational reference plant for the new reactor design, sharing the cost of building a FOAK nuclear power plant with the utility buyer.  Any losses from this LSTK contract may be considered a vendor investment in product development for a FOAK reactor design.  Profits on subsequent projects using the same design with lower costs due to learning may justify a nuclear power plant vendor to use the LSTK approach.

A nuclear power plant vendor may also use an LSTK contract to secure a strategic position in the market.  Offering a power plant with attractive LSTK terms may convince a buyer to commit, blocking competing vendors.

The future sale of nuclear fuel, replacement parts, and services for a new nuclear power plant may cover any losses due to selling a nuclear power plant sale with LSTK terms (i.e., AREVA's so-called Nespresso Strategy).[33]

The LSTK contract approach offers a simpler contractual approach, giving the nuclear power plant vendor more control over the nuclear power plant procurement and construction process.[34]

### *Financial Capability to Meet LSTK Requirements*

A key issue is whether a nuclear power plant buyer can rely on a nuclear power plant vendor to take all completion risk under an LSTK contract.  A nuclear power plant vendor may not have the financial capability to take losses if the project does not go smoothly.

Westinghouse sold two nuclear power plant projects in the US with LSTK contracts, one at the Vogtle site in Georgia and one at the V.C. Summer site in South Carolina.  These LSTK contracts led to Westinghouse losses when the nuclear plant projects experienced cost overruns, with Westinghouse filing for bankruptcy in 2017.  The Westinghouse bankruptcy led to the abandonment of the V.C. Summer plant project in 2017 and a restructuring of the Vogtle plant project.[35]

The LSTK contract for the Olkiluoto 3 nuclear power plant in Finland has led to large financial losses for the nuclear power plant vendor, AREVA.[36] A key difference between this project and the Westinghouse US projects is that AREVA had the French government's financial backing. The Olkiluoto 3 project is moving toward completion despite large losses for the vendor.

Like AREVA, state-owned nuclear vendors have the financial capability to accept nuclear power plant completion risk and potential financial losses from selling nuclear power plants using the LSTK approach.

State-owned nuclear vendors may justify losses under an LSTK contract by importing nuclear power industry jobs to their home country and pursuing national geopolitical interests by selling nuclear power plants.

### *Vendor-Led IPP to address*
### *Completion Risk*

An alternative to large potential losses when selling a nuclear power plant using the LSTK approach is for the nuclear power plant vendor to develop and build its own nuclear IPP.

The HPC nuclear power project in the UK is an example of a vendor-led nuclear power IPP project. HPC will sell its output into the British electricity market with a government-sponsored long-term power contract to hedge electricity market prices and lower revenue risk for the project. EDF, a French nuclear industrial company and nuclear utility, is the owner, builder, and operator of the project. The HPC project provides EDF with an opportunity to draw upon EPR reactor experience in Finland, China, and France and help keep the French nuclear power supply chain intact. The HPC project also has significant investment by a Chinese state-owned nuclear industrial company, China General Nuclear Power Group (CGN). CGN's HPC investment was conditional on UK government approval to build a Chinese nuclear power at the Bradwell site.

The Akkuyu BOO project in Turkey is another example of a vendor-led nuclear power IPP project. Akkuyu has power contracts with Turkish government utilities for some of its output, with the remaining output sold into the Turkish electricity market. Akkuyu will be built, owned, and operated by Rosatom, a Russian state-owned nuclear industrial company.

Several nuclear IPPs developed by private nuclear vendors have failed to move to the construction phase. In the UK, two major shareholder-owned nuclear industrial companies (i.e., Toshiba and Hitachi) declined to invest in the NuGeneration and Horizon nuclear IPPs, even after they spent substantial amounts for project development. The Sinop nuclear IPP (BOO) project in Turkey, with shareholder-owned Mitsubishi as the lead investor, was canceled. A key issue with these projects was the financial risk associated with assuming project completion risk.

### Revenue Risk

Revenue risk is the risk that revenue from the sale of power will not cover generating costs and provide a return on investment.

In the traditional approach, the regulated or government utility recovers the cost of building and operating the nuclear power plant. End-use electricity customers, and maybe taxpayers, pay for this, but they receive benefits from the nuclear power plant.

In the nuclear IPP model, the nuclear power plant owner/operator sells electricity to produce the revenue to recover investment and cover generating costs. In some instances, this revenue comes from a power purchase agreement or other power contracts. In other instances, this revenue comes from the sale of nuclear electricity into an electricity market, perhaps with supplemental revenue from capacity markets or other items. The uncertainty about whether a nuclear IPP revenue will be sufficient to recover investment and cover generating costs is revenue risk. Revenue risk is a concern because some merchant nuclear power plants do not earn enough electricity sale revenue to cover generating costs, much less a return on investment.

### Vertical Integration

The traditional model uses vertical integration and recovery of costs from end-use customers in regulated rates to provide long-term revenue certainty for nuclear power projects. In addition to increased revenue certainty, vertical integration may offer other benefits to traditional utilities.

### *Power Contracts*

In some traditional nuclear power projects, a full requirements power contract is used. In these contracts, an electricity buyer takes a share of nuclear power plant output and pays a share of nuclear power plant costs. A full requirements contract has a financial impact like ownership of the nuclear power plant. One example of these contracts is seen in the Finnish Mankala company approach used for several existing and proposed nuclear power projects, where the agreement between the participants and the Mankala company resembling a full requirements power contract. Other examples are the participation agreements related to jointly-owned US nuclear power plants[37] and the power purchase agreements between Entergy's Grand Gulf nuclear power station and affiliated regulated electric utilities in several states.

Some IPPs rely on power contracts or power purchase agreements (PPAs) for revenue certainty. These power contracts typically include stipulated prices (i.e., rather than the pass-through of actual costs in full requirements contracts). PPA prices may be based on negotiations, an auction process, or an administrative process (e.g., utility avoided cost estimates). Stipulated price power contract prices are set before the contract is signed and before an IPP project is developed and placed into operation. If project capital or operating costs are higher than expected, the project may be less profitable than expected.

PPAs are used in bilateral markets, where utilities use PPAs to obtain wholesale electricity for resale to end-use customers.

In electricity spot markets, a power contract is likely to be a contract for differences (CfD). A CfD is a two-way, single-price hedge agreement between two parties participating in an electricity spot market. A CfD includes a quantity of power and a strike price. The seller, typically a generator participating in the spot market, sells electricity into the spot market. The buyer, typically a utility with end-use customers, buys power in the spot market. If the spot price is above the CfD strike price, the seller pays the buyer the difference between the spot price and the strike price. If the spot price is below the CfD strike price, the buyer pays the seller the difference between the strike price and the spot price. CfD contracts are financial contracts outside the spot market that use the spot market price as a reference point for CfD difference payments.

### Other industry organization issues

The nuclear power industry organization also has implications for transaction costs, fleet build efficiencies, and national nuclear programs.

### Transaction Costs

The nuclear power industry faces high transaction and coordination costs. Nuclear power plants are large and complex projects, and multiple parties must expend effort and resources to negotiate complicated agreements with high financial value and high risk as a part of a nuclear build project. High transaction costs result when private parties in a nuclear power project are engaged using bilateral commercial contracts.

In a country with state-owned electricity and nuclear power industries, the national government is the single economic entity that owns and controls the electricity industry, nuclear industrial suppliers, and nuclear power projects. A nuclear power project has a government nuclear power plant vendor and nuclear power project owner and operator that delivers electricity to a government electric utility. Transactions and coordination costs among the different entities may be low because they are all part of the government. A planned economy nuclear power plant program may have lower transaction costs and more flexibility in execution.

In the US and other market economies, the same activities occur, but the entities doing these activities are separate shareholder-owned, profit-seeking, risk-managing private companies. Each transaction is the result of a complicated and expensive procurement and tendering process. Sellers must decide on a price and a level of risk, and buyers seek information from multiple sellers to determine the best deal for them. Separate consulting or engineering firms may be retained to manage procurement, project activity, and other activities. Each transaction has a contract, drafted and reviewed by law firms, that spells out the transaction details, defines the risks and responsibilities for each party, and establishes the consequences of faulty products or delayed deliveries.

Nuclear power plant investors, lenders, and owners may be different from the companies building the nuclear power plant and different from the utility buying the electricity produced by the nuclear power plant. This approach leads to higher transaction costs, less flexibility in the project execution, and, typically, more commercial disputes than government nuclear projects.

### *Fleet Build*

Investing in a large fleet of nuclear power plants is a substantial undertaking that may bring significant benefits.

Fleet build can reduce completion risk, lower cost, and shorten build schedules after the initial units are completed. A proven way to lower completion risk is to build multiple nuclear power plants with the same design and a sequential construction approach in a series build program. Lessons learned during the first nuclear power plant construction lowers capital cost and time to build for additional units. A well-developed nuclear fleet build program can reliably lower nuclear power plant cost and completion time.

A national nuclear fleet build program's potential benefits are greater if the planned nuclear fleet is large.

### *National Nuclear Power Industry*

Several countries, including France, China, and Russia, have shown that a government approach to nuclear power can result in large and successful nuclear power programs. These countries have government-owned electric utilities that own and operate nuclear power plants and have government-owned nuclear industrial companies.

France has very low electricity sector carbon emissions because nuclear power is its primary electricity generation source. France also exports clean nuclear electricity to other countries in Europe, helping these countries control their electricity sector carbon emissions.

China and Russia have growing nuclear power fleets. The domestic nuclear power programs in these countries provide their state-owned nuclear industrial companies with proven reactor designs and supply chains that support the world's nuclear power market.

With large orders from affiliated government electric utilities, government-owned nuclear vendors can develop an integrated nuclear supply chain, invest in human resources, and invest in manufacturing capacity based on long production runs. The government captures benefits from learning-by-doing and mass production from building multiple identical nuclear power plants through declining plant costs. This approach results in national nuclear champions competing in the global nuclear power market based on experience and proven results in their home market.

State-owned nuclear power industrial companies already dominate the global nuclear power market. Countries that want to build a new nuclear power program may become clients of a state-owned nuclear vendor rather than developing a domestic nuclear power industry from scratch. Investor-owned nuclear industrial companies may not compete successfully with state-owned nuclear vendors that can accept nuclear power project completion risk and provide client countries with financing options.

Also, in a market economy with multiple competing nuclear power plant vendors, a nuclear fleet build approach may not be feasible. Competing nuclear power plant vendors and designs may mean that it is difficult for any single vendor, builder, or reactor design to achieve the level of learning seen in a coordinated national nuclear fleet build program. Also, the very large investment required for a nuclear fleet build approach may only be feasible with government ownership.

Nuclear fleet build programs can provide the basis for a country to establish national nuclear power industrial capacity. A country may use a nuclear fleet build program to support its nuclear industrial development strategy and create a national nuclear power champion.

France did this in its nuclear build-out in the 1970s and 1980s, and China is doing this today.[38]

Selling nuclear power plants or nuclear power goods and services in the export market is a way to import nuclear sector jobs back to a state-owned nuclear vendor's home country.[39]

# Insights

Nuclear power has a unique set of economic and technical attributes that make it a valuable resource. However, these attributes make nuclear power projects inconsistent with a deregulated electricity industry and electricity markets.

Government and regulated electric utilities consider new power plant investments by examining current and long-term projected demand, system reliability, total system cost, and end-user electricity rates. These utilities, and their economic regulator, may also consider social and public good issues, including environmental impact, local and regional jobs, local and regional tax revenue, and the impact on local communities. Nuclear power typically fares well against other generating technologies in this approach.

A nuclear IPP, BOO, or merchant nuclear project is evaluated on financial outcomes from project costs and revenue. Nuclear power does not fare well in this type of financial evaluation. If nuclear power projects, evaluated like any other privately-owned unregulated electricity generation project, will almost certainly be dominated by lower-capital intensity, faster-to-build, high-marginal-cost power plants like natural gas power plants.

The next chapter covers the approaches to the electricity industry and how nuclear power fits into these approaches.

# ELECTRICITY

*"Finding a way for nuclear power to work in liberalized electricity markets is one of the biggest problems facing the electricity industry - and the nuclear power industry - today."*

Edward Kee - *Can nuclear succeed in liberalized electricity markets?*[40]

Nuclear power plants generate electricity, with the electricity industry determining the value of electricity and nuclear power value.

The electricity industry started over a century ago with small on-site power plants that were owned and operated by local electricity users. The industry evolved into today's widespread network of high-voltage transmission lines linking large power plants to load centers.

The electricity industry was dominated by vertically-integrated government and regulated utilities (i.e., the traditional approach) until the 1990s when some countries deregulated their electricity industry and established electricity markets (i.e., the new approach).

The electricity industry approach has a profound influence on power plant value and investment decisions. There are clear indications that the new electricity industry approach is not compatible with nuclear power.

This chapter provides an overview of how the electricity industry is organized and how wholesale power systems operate. Readers may want to do additional reading on these topics. [41]

## Industry Organization

The traditional electricity industry approach has been in place for more than a century and remains in many parts of the world today. The new electricity industry approach was developed and implemented during and after the 1990s.

### Traditional Approach

*"Prior to the 1990s, most electricity customers in the US were served by regulated, vertically-integrated, monopoly utilities that handled electricity generation, transmission, local distribution and billing/collections. Regulators set retail electricity prices to allow the utility to recover its prudently incurred costs, a process known as cost-of-service regulation."*

Severin Borenstein and James Bushnell -
*The U.S. Electricity Industry after 20 Years of Restructuring*[42]

In the traditional approach, vertically-integrated electric utilities provide electricity to end-use customers. Utilities provide this service by planning, investing in, operating, and maintaining an electricity system to meet customer demand with a high degree of reliability. This electricity system includes power plants, transmission lines, local distribution lines, and other infrastructure. The cost of building and operating the electricity system is recovered from electricity users in rates (i.e., prices) for electricity service. Traditional utilities may be regulated investor-owned utilities, government-owned utilities, or public power utilities.

Regulated investor-owned electric utilities are shareholder-owned firms with a monopoly electricity service area and an obligation to serve all customers in this service area. An economic regulator oversees regulated utility rates, investment decisions, and other matters.

Government-owned electric utilities (e.g., municipal utilities) are similar, with the government overseeing rates and investment decisions. Government-owned electric utilities are typical in centrally-planned economies but are also present in some market economies.

Public power utilities (e.g., cooperatives) are tax-exempt companies that provide electricity at cost to members.

In the US, tax-exempt government and public power utilities are non-profit entities that provide cost-based electricity service to their customers and co-exist with traditional electric utilities and electricity markets.

Traditional utilities provide reliable electricity service to end users while minimizing the long-term total cost of this service. Traditional utilities plan and invest in power plants, transmission lines, distribution lines, and other infrastructure. They may also purchase wholesale power from other utilities or private power plants. System investment decisions made by traditional utilities are based on cost, along with other issues, including system reliability, environmental impacts, economic impacts, industrial development, jobs, and other public goods. These investment decisions are reviewed and approved by governments and economic regulators.

Traditional power plant investments are supported by arrangements to recover capital investments, debt service, and generating costs from ratepayers. In government utilities, ratepayer revenue may be supplemented by taxpayers. Traditional utilities power plant investments are supported by a high degree of certainty that the investment will be recovered.

The long-term revenue certainty in the traditional approach supports investment in long-lived capital-intensive power plant projects, including nuclear and hydroelectric power plants. Traditional utilities, and the economic regulators that oversee them, can make infrastructure investment decisions for the long term (e.g., 60 years or longer).

More than a century of successful experience with the traditional approach led to investment in an extensive network of transmission lines, power plants, and other electricity industry infrastructure.

There are several important differences between the traditional approach and the new approach. The new approach does not have long-term planning of power plants, little consideration of power plants' public-good attributes, and provides little revenue certainty to support power plant investments.

### New Approach

*"Electricity market restructuring is widely seen as having failed."*

Lester Lave, Jay Apt, and Seth Blumsack -
*Deregulation / Restructuring Part I:*
*Reregulation will not fix the problems*[43]

Reforms of the traditional electricity industry approach started in the early 1990s in some countries.

Several factors drove electricity industry reform.[44] The Thatcher and Reagan governments deregulated and marketized other industries (e.g., natural gas, airlines, and telecommunications) in the UK and US, providing a precedent for electricity sector reform. A new non-utility independent power sector provided a viable alternative to traditional utility ownership of power plants. Computer software and hardware needed to manage real-time electricity system dispatch using bid-based spot markets became available.

Electricity reform involves the de-integration of traditional electric utilities, splitting vertically-integrated utilities into separate power plant companies, regulated transmission and distribution companies, and retail electricity suppliers. Electricity reform requires new wholesale electricity markets and new independent entities to operate these electricity markets and the wholesale power system (i.e., Independent Market and System Operators).

In the new approach, wholesale electricity generated by deregulated or merchant power plants is sold into a wholesale electricity market, with electricity retailers buying electricity from these markets.

An important difference between this new approach and the traditional approach is how power plants are planned. In the new approach, market-based power plant investment is expected to replace the traditional approach to generation planning and investment. The new approach assumes that electricity market prices will result in investments in new power plants. There has been some investment in new merchant power plants, but most deregulated power plants were built as regulated power plants by pre-reform traditional utilities, then divested or privatized as required by electricity industry reforms.

The traditional approach has utilities and economic regulators that consider a range of public-good power plant attributes and system outcomes when making power plant and electricity system investment decisions. The new approach focuses on power plant cash flow from commodity bulk electricity sales that do not reflect public goods.

The long-term recovery of power plant investment in the traditional approach is replaced by uncertain electricity market revenue in the new approach. Wholesale electricity market prices may not cover the generating costs for some existing power plants (e.g., nuclear power) and may not provide sufficient incentives for necessary and appropriate system power plant investment. Long-term investments in nuclear power in the new approach are unlikely to happen without added long-term revenue certainty from outside electricity spot markets.

The experience to date with the new approach is mixed. New wholesale electricity markets manage the dispatch of power plants as well as or better than utility-level dispatch in the traditional approach.

However, it is unclear that electricity markets will deliver the generation capacity needed for reliable service or that a market-based generation mix will minimize long-term total system costs. Electricity spot markets have led to capacity markets, reliability requirements imposed on load-serving entities, and other government interventions to address these shortcomings.

The failure of electricity markets to deliver adequate and appropriate generation sector investments has strong negative implications for nuclear power.

# Wholesale Electricity

*"Taken in its entirety, the [electricity] grid is a machine, the most complex machine ever made. The National Academy of Engineering called it the greatest engineering achievement of the 20th century. It represents the largest industrial investment in history."*

Phillip Schewe - *The Grid: A Journey Through the Heart of Our Electrified World*[45]

The complex wholesale electricity system, referred to as the electricity grid or the bulk power system, is a network of high-voltage transmission lines, power plants, load centers, and other infrastructure. The same bulk power system features are present in both electricity industry approaches.

In the traditional approach, a regulated or government utility recovers wholesale electricity costs (i.e., the cost of owning and operating power plants or buying wholesale power from other utilities) from ratepayers or taxpayers. Utility revenue covers all power plant costs, including debt service and a return on investment for investor-owned regulated utilities.

In the new approach, wholesale electricity markets use power plant bids to determine the system dispatch and spot prices that determine merchant power plant revenue from selling electricity into the spot market. Some merchant power plants may not be financially viable in this approach. In the US, merchant nuclear plants have closed due to financial losses from operations in an electricity market.

### *System Dispatch*

Electricity demand varies over hours, days, weeks, and years. Time-varying electricity demand is met by power plant output in real time by turning on (and loading up) power plants when demand increases and by doing the opposite when demand decreases.[46] The process of adjusting power plant output to meet real-time electricity demand is called system dispatch. Economic system dispatch is based on power plant short-run marginal cost (SRMC).

SRMC is the change in total power plant cost due to a small change in power plant output over a short period. For example, if the total power plant cost is $5 higher when power plant output increases from 1,000 MW to 1,001 MW for an hour, then the SRMC of that additional MWh is $5/MWh.

SRMC does not include fixed generating costs, debt service, or a return on investment.[47] The SRMC for combustion-based power plants is based on fuel costs because more fuel is used to generate each additional MWh. The SRMC of nuclear, hydroelectric, and renewable power plants is zero because generating costs are fixed and do not change with short-term output changes.

Economic system dispatch involves dispatching power plants in order of SRMC, subject to system constraints (e.g., transmission line capacity and reliability contingency requirements). Available power plants with low SRMC are operated first, with higher-SRMC power plants dispatched as needed to meet additional demand. SRMC-based economic system dispatch minimizes system marginal cost.

In the traditional approach, economic system dispatch is done by vertically-integrated utilities using SRMC estimates. Traditional utilities dispatch power plants to minimize system marginal costs and recover all power plant costs (i.e., marginal and fixed costs) from ratepayers.

In the new approach, economic system dispatch is done by market clearing software that evaluates SRMC-based power plant bids. For each trading period (e.g., a half-hour), market-clearing software sorts bids by SRMC. The lowest-SRMC bids are accepted first, then higher-SRMC bids are accepted until the total electricity from all accepted bids meets demand in the trading period, as shown in Figure 8.

In both the traditional and new approaches, power plants with low or zero SRMC operate as much as possible.

All power plants with accepted bids operate and sell their output at the same system spot price in these electricity markets.

## Figure 8 - Electricity Market Price

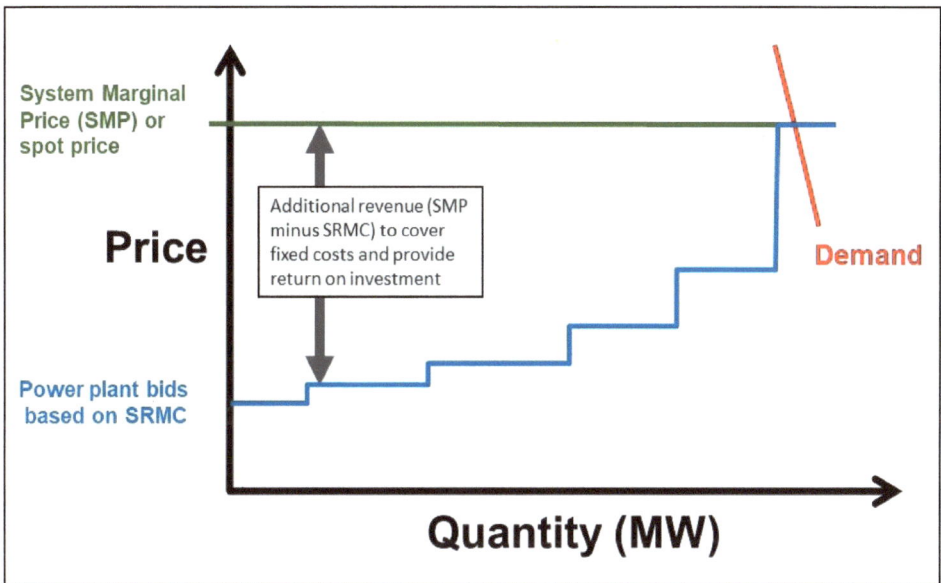

### *Spot Market Prices*

In the traditional approach, there is no electricity spot market price.

In the new approach, the highest-SRMC bid accepted (i.e., the marginal bid) in a trading period sets the system marginal price (SMP) for that trading period. SMP is often referred to as the spot price. All power plants with accepted bids operate and sell electricity to the market operator at the same system spot price, regardless of their bid or SRMC, as shown in the green line in Figure 8. Many electricity markets have locational spot pricing, so that the spot price may be different at each location in the system.

The spot price is based on SRMC-based bids, so electricity sales at the system spot price are sure to cover marginal generating costs for each power plant with accepted bids in a trading period. However, the marginal bidder that sets the spot price in a trading period only gets paid the spot price and will only cover its marginal costs. The marginal unit in a trading period earns no additional revenue to cover fixed costs or investment returns.

All accepted bidders other than the marginal bidder (i.e., the inframarginal bidders) are paid the same spot price as the marginal bidder. The spot price is higher than inframarginal bids, providing net revenue based on the difference between the spot price and each bidder's SRMC, as shown in Figure 8. The lower a power plant's SRMC, the higher the additional net revenue will be. The additional net revenue received by inframarginal bidders helps them pay for fixed generating costs, debt service, and a return on investment.

In electricity markets, power plant dispatch and spot price changes in each trading period, so the inframarginal set of power plants and the additional net revenue they receive changes in each trading period.

### *Spot Market Revenue*

*"Although it might be possible to raise capital on reasonable terms to build base-load generating plants that would not be insulated by long-term contracts from the natural risk of the bulk power marketplace, we find it hard to imagine that base-load power plants anything like those we see today would be constructed in the face of the extreme additional opportunism risks inherent in a regime permitting only spot market sales."*

Paul L Joskow and Richard Schmalensee -
*Markets for Power, An Analysis of Electric
Utility Deregulation*[48]

In the traditional approach, total system costs that include all fixed and marginal power plant costs are recovered in customer rates. In the new approach, electricity spot market sales make up most merchant power plant revenue, with some additional revenue coming from capacity markets, hedge agreements, government incentives, tax credits, and other sources.

The total annual spot market revenue for a merchant power plant is not certain to cover fixed generating costs or a return on investment. The potential shortfall in revenue from spot market sales is an issue for all merchant power plants but is a serious problem for power plants with high fixed generating costs like nuclear power plants. Nuclear power plants have experienced financial losses in electricity markets.

Accordingly, factors that influence spot prices have an important influence on merchant nuclear power plant revenue. These factors include fossil fuel prices, intermittent generation, demand levels, generator bidding constraints, and market rules that allow negative prices.

### *Fossil Fuel Prices*

Electricity market spot prices are strongly linked to fossil fuel prices because fossil-fuel power plants are the marginal unit in most electricity market trading periods. The SRMC of these marginal units is based on marginal fuel cost, so fossil fuel prices greatly influence electricity spot market prices.

Natural gas is the fuel for many marginal fossil fuel power plants. Natural gas market prices have been low in the US for some time, resulting in lower spot prices and lower electricity market revenue for all inframarginal units. Low natural gas market prices in the US have reduced electricity market spot prices and resulted in lower revenue and financial losses for nuclear power plants operating in electricity markets.

### *Intermittent Renewable Generation*

Electricity market spot prices are also influenced by the type and amount of renewable generation participating in the market.

Renewable (e.g., wind and solar) power plant intermittent output is determined by uncertain and uncontrollable wind and sun. The SRMC of renewable generation is zero, like nuclear power.

Renewable generation investment is largely based on out-of-market incentives, including federal tax credits and state renewable mandates, unlike other merchant power plant projects that rely on electricity market revenue. Renewable electricity generation investments may be made even if electricity market prices do not signal a need for new capacity. When system demand growth is low or flat, adding new renewable generation capacity pushes the entire market supply curve to the right and lowers the spot price.

Even worse, renewable generation incentives may be paid based on physical output (e.g., production tax credits or feed-in tariffs). Renewable production tax credits are paid for electricity generated, regardless of location, trading period, or electricity value.

Output-based incentives like production tax credits reduce the SRMC of the generator receiving the incentive. The production tax credit adds a marginal benefit, instead of a marginal cost, for electricity generated. A renewable generator with an SRMC of zero will have a negative SRMC when output-based incentives are received. If allowed by market rules, these renewable generators may submit bids with negative prices (i.e., the renewable generator is willing to pay the market operator when it runs). Such negative bids will be at the bottom of the economic dispatch stack and will be selected first.

Adding renewable generation with zero or negative bids means that the supply curve in Figure 8 is pushed to the right. When the supply curve is moved to the right, spot prices are lower because lower-SRMC bids are on the margin. In market trading periods with a lot of renewable energy available (e.g., a windy night or a sunny day), renewable energy may provide a substantial portion of system demand, resulting in very low spot market prices. Renewable generation may even be on the margin in some trading periods, making the spot market price zero or negative.

### *Demand Levels*

When system demand is low, electricity spot market prices are low because lower-SRMC bidders are on the margin. System demand is based on the total amount of electricity used by customers in each trading period. Customer electricity use may be lower because of more efficient homes or appliances. Low demand may also result from an economic downturn, a regional shift away from industrial activity, milder weather than expected (e.g., a cool summer or a warm winter), or other factors.

Another reason for lower net system demand is that customers may install local power generation connected behind the utility electricity meter. A rooftop solar panel system connected to an electricity customer's house (i.e., on the customer side of the utility meter) means that solar panel output results in lower system demand. High penetration of rooftop solar panels may result in substantial demand reduction when the sun is shining. This demand reduction means a lower need for wholesale power generation and lower, or even negative, spot market prices.

Solar energy requires reliable electricity to meet system demand when solar output is not available. These gaps are in the morning when system demand increases before solar output ramps up and in the late afternoon when solar output drops off when the sun goes down.

An example of the effect of solar generation is seen in the California electricity market. The California daily net load is low (i.e., there is a reduced need for generation) in mid-day due to high solar panel output.[49] Flexible and reliable power plants are needed to balance the system. This flexible generation, typically using natural gas fuel, must quickly reduce output in the morning when solar generation increases and quickly increase output at the end of the day when solar generation output decreases. The end of the day is a more significant problem in California, as the electricity demand to run air conditioning on hot sunny days continues for several hours after the sun has set, and solar unit output is gone. In the California electricity market, solar power means that spot prices are low or negative in the middle of the day.

Another example is South Australia, which had enough solar power at noon on 11 October 2020 to meet all state electricity demand.[50] Excess power, from wind generation and gas-fired generation required for ancillary services, was exported to other Australian states via high-voltage transmission interconnections. Electricity spot prices in South Australia were negative during this event.

### *Power Plant Bidding Constraints*

Power plants are constrained by physical limits, including minimum generation levels, ramp rate limits, the time required to restart after a shutdown, and other constraints. These constraints mean that bids into an electricity market are more complex than simple combinations of output and bid price.

Some generators bid into electricity markets as price takers. A price taker bid does not set the market price, enables the bidder (i.e., all or part of a power plant) to operate without being dispatched off by the market operator, and means that the power plant is paid at the spot market price in each trading period.

Power plants, including nuclear power plants, submit price taker bids when they do not want to operate flexibly in the electricity market. For example, fossil-fuel power plants have a minimum generation level (e.g., no lower than 40% of rated capacity without shutting down) and may submit a price-taker bid for their output at the minimum generation level.

Nuclear power plants submit price-taker bids to ensure that they operate at full output between refueling outages.

Cogeneration power plants that co-produce electricity and heat energy may be required to provide heat energy even if the electricity spot price is low or negative, leading to the use of price-taker bids.

Less obvious are price taker bids from power plants with out-of-market bilateral power contracts that restrict generator physical output and power plants required for ancillary services.

If there are enough price taker bids, the result may be negative spot market prices.

### Negative Prices

Negative spot prices are allowed in most electricity markets. When spot markets are negative in a trading period, all generators selling power into the market in that trading period pay to deliver power. Negative prices should increase demand (i.e., customers are paid to use electricity) and decrease generator output.

Negative prices happen when the total amount of inflexible generator bids is higher than the demand for electricity in a trading period. When this happens, the market price is lowered until generators withdraw, if possible, to reduce supply and price-sensitive users increase demand. A negative market price may be needed to balance supply and demand in the market.

Nuclear power plants are usually operated at full output during all hours between refueling outages so that a negative spot price means that the nuclear power plant operator must make payments to the market operator and incur operating losses.

# Power Plant Investment Decisions

*"Moreover, large infrastructure projects can have long lifespans and for typical discount rate values, the conventional DCF implies that anything that happens after 20 years becomes irrelevant. Thus, the effect of DCF-led valuations is that they favour short-term gains at the expense of future generations - the method simply presents as unattractive any investment whose advantages might take a bit longer to emerge."*

Arturo Cifuentes and David Espinoza -
*Infrastructure investing and the peril of discounted cash flow*[51]

The differences between the traditional and new electricity industry approaches have profound implications for power plant investments, especially nuclear power plant investments.

It requires about ten years and billions of dollars in project investment to build a nuclear power plant that will operate for 60 to 100 years. The large financial commitment, long construction period, and long asset life make a nuclear power plant investment more difficult than other power plant investments.

In addition to the large size, long development period, and long operating life, market-based nuclear power projects face additional hurdles due to a lack of revenue certainty, the financial evaluation process, and completion risk.

### *Revenue Certainty*

In the traditional approach, a regulated or government utility makes power plant investments a part of a long-term power plant and system planning process, with oversight and approval from economic regulators or government owners. With a high degree of certainty about how a power plant investment will be recovered, regulated asset treatment supports debt and equity funding for traditional utility power plant investments.

In the new approach, market-based power plant investments are based on projected revenue and profits from selling electricity into the spot market. Uncertain spot market prices and power plant dispatch levels provide little revenue certainty. The high level of revenue risk for market-based power plants makes investment and financing of any power plant difficult. This revenue risk makes a market-based nuclear power plant investment virtually impossible.

### *Financial Evaluation*

Market-based power plant projects are evaluated using discounted cash flow (DCF) analysis. In DCF analyses, project net cash flow (i.e., revenues minus costs) is estimated over the project's life. Future cash flows are discounted to the present using an appropriate discount rate. Annual discounted cash flows are added together to get the project's net present value

(NPV). Cash flows more than about 30 years in the future have a very low value when discounted and contribute little to project NPV. This discounting approach ignores cash flows after about 30 years for long-lived power technologies like nuclear power.

There are serious shortcomings of DCF analyses for nuclear power projects.

The first 30 years of a nuclear power plant project includes the large negative cash flow during the first ten years (i.e., during the development and construction period). The negative cash flows in the first ten years greatly impact NPV because these cash flows are discounted less than the positive cash flows that occur after construction is completed.

Positive cash flows for the first 20 years of nuclear power plant commercial operation are included, but the positive cash flows from nuclear operation for the remainder of the nuclear power plant's long operating life (i.e., 60 years or longer) add little to the project's NPV.

Investors prefer projects with higher NPVs, which means a preference for power plant investments with shorter construction periods and lower initial capital costs, even if these power plants have high fuel and operating costs. In the new electricity industry approach, market-based power plant investment will focus on project NPV rather than on the project's impact on long-term public goods or long-run total electricity costs.

The Levelized Cost of Electricity (LCOE) measure is also based on discounted project cash flows. There are also serious shortcomings with LCOE analyses.[52] LCOE is a useful preliminary measure to compare new generation options, but significant additional analysis is needed.

LCOE analysis starts with estimating annual project cash flows and electricity output to develop annual electricity costs (i.e., in units of $/MWh). LCOE is calculated as an annual cost of electricity that is the same every year (i.e., levelized), but with the same NPV as the variable annual electricity cost. LCOE analyses embed critical assumptions about generating costs and capacity factors that, along with discount rates, should be carefully considered when using LCOE estimates.

No nuclear power plants have been built under the new electricity industry approach unless there are substantial out-of-market incentives and other factors. The new Hinkley Point C nuclear project in the UK electricity market has an out-of-market long-term power contract that provides revenue certainty and is being developed by state-owned nuclear industrial companies with strategic and geopolitical reasons for investing (i.e., EDF Energy and CGN).

Market-based power plant investment decisions are based on financial evaluation tools that inherently disadvantage nuclear power projects. Merchant nuclear power project investments in these electricity markets, absent substantial intervention, are unlikely.

### *Completion Risk*

Completion risk for nuclear power plants is a large and important issue. Historically, completion risk has been assumed by government or investor-owned regulated utilities in the traditional electricity industry approach. Apportioning completion risk in the new approach is a difficult issue that has yet to be resolved.

In planned economies with nuclear power, the government owns and controls both the electricity industry and the nuclear power industry. The government makes decisions about nuclear power plant investments by government-owned utilities and decides how completion risk is managed. These countries have state-owned utilities buying nuclear power plants from national nuclear industrial companies that may also compete globally. A domestic nuclear power plant build program is usually part of a national energy and industrial development strategy in these countries and may justify decisions that place significant completion risk on government nuclear power plant vendors or government utility buyers.

For regulated investor-owned utilities in countries with a market economy, laws, regulations, and regulator decisions determine how or if the regulated utility invests in a nuclear power plant. A critical aspect is how nuclear project completion risk is shared between customers and regulated utility shareholders. Investor-owned regulated utility investor preferences will reflect the US experience with nuclear power project disallowances (i.e., utility shareholders were not allowed to recover some nuclear power project costs from customers). Only a few new US regulated nuclear power plant project investments were made in recent years, and these were in states where laws and electricity regulations were favorable to nuclear power and utility investors (e.g., the Vogtle expansion project in Georgia).

In the new approach, with market-based nuclear power plant projects, one of the most important issues is apportioning completion risk, as discussed in the previous chapter. So far, government involvement has been needed to manage completion risk in market-based nuclear projects.

# Climate Change

The electricity sector is a major contributor to global climate change. Some electricity industry features make it a near-term target for reducing emissions of carbon and other greenhouse gases.

Clean nuclear electricity can reduce the substantial amounts of carbon dioxide and other air pollutants generated by combustion-based generation in the electricity sector.

In the traditional approach, the government or economic regulator can decide to close carbon dioxide-emitting generators and replace them with generators that do not emit carbon dioxide. Governments and utility economic regulators can place a cost on combustion-based power plant air emissions, increasing the value of zero-emission nuclear power. Governments and economic utility regulators can recognize public goods like clean air in the generation expansion planning process, and the cost of actions to maximize these public goods can be recovered in electricity rates and taxes.

In the new approach, the decarbonization of the electricity industry is more difficult and less certain. Electricity systems based on electricity markets may have no power plant planning process, relying on market-based power plant entry and exit. Market-based power plant entry and exit depend on profitability in the electricity market, rather than reducing air emissions or providing other public goods. Readily available low-cost fossil fuels, along with less risky and less expensive combustion-based power plants, are likely to result in a higher amount of combustion-based generation and higher electricity sector carbon emissions in electricity markets.

In the new approach, mechanisms outside of the electricity market (e.g., carbon taxes, regulations, and renewable subsidies) must be used to tilt the market toward low or zero-carbon generation options. These mechanisms may reduce electricity sector carbon emissions but may have unintended consequences, like the system reliability issues created by intermittent renewable generation that require fossil fuel generation to maintain system reliability and increase air emissions.

Electricity market dispatch and price-setting algorithms may not work well in a decarbonized electricity system. The electricity market design assumes that SRMC-based bids will be submitted with increasing price levels (i.e., an upward-sloping supply curve). The classic generation supply curve is composed of positive generator bids with prices that increase at increasing total generation levels, as represented by the blue line in Figure 8.[53] Combustion-based power plants are the marginal units in many trading periods and set the spot price for all participants.

Most existing electricity markets have a portfolio of power plants that include combustion-based power plants. A zero-carbon electricity system would have no fossil fuel power plants. Power plants with no carbon dioxide emissions (e.g., nuclear power, hydroelectric, and renewables) also have marginal costs that are zero or negative (i.e., because of output-based out-of-market incentives). Electricity market algorithms used to dispatch power plants based on bids may not work well when all power plants bid at zero or negative levels.

Even if electricity markets can manage dispatch, electricity market spot prices will be zero or negative, and power plants selling into the market will have little or no electricity spot market revenue. All power plant revenue will come from outside the spot market. This out-of-market revenue, determined by factors other than the spot market, will determine the profitability and continued operation of existing power plants and provide revenue for new power plant investments.

Electricity markets might be developed that will function in systems with a large amount of zero-SRMC generation resources.[54] However, the recent experience in Australia, California, and other markets show the difficulty of operating electricity markets with large penetration of renewable generation.

Decarbonizing the electricity sector may be more difficult in the new approach, and the new electricity markets may not work in a zero-carbon electricity system.

The traditional electricity industry approach is more compatible with nuclear power and may allow faster and more effective decarbonization of the electricity sector.

## Implications

*"Early retirement of existing nuclear power plants and the failure to build new nuclear power plants during this period of low electricity prices results in the loss of substantial electricity system, economic, and environmental public benefits. This is a failure of the US market approach to nuclear power."*

Edward Kee - *NECG Commentary #14 – Market Failure and Nuclear power*[55]

*"There is a concern that competitive electricity markets may not trigger investments in large, high fixed-cost projects with long lead time such as nuclear . . . "*

International Energy Agency - *2014 Energy Policy Review of the United States*[56]

All nuclear power plants operating today, and almost all nuclear power plants under construction today, were built by a traditional government or regulated utility.

The evidence indicates that nuclear power is not compatible with deregulated electricity markets. Electricity markets do not provide long-term revenue certainty to justify investment in a nuclear power project. New merchant nuclear power plant investments are possible, but only if there is a substantial intervention in the market (e.g., the HPC project in the UK and the Bruce Power nuclear refurbishment project in Ontario).

Climate change is an issue that may drive countries to reject a market-based approach to electricity because it makes it difficult or impossible to develop nuclear power.

# MARKET FAILURE

*"When merchant nuclear power plants are threatened with closure, you should think about market failure and ways to stop market failure to preserve the public benefits of nuclear power."*

Edward Kee - *NECG Commentary #21 – Market Failure*[57]

Market failure related to the nuclear power and electricity industry is the focus of this book.

## Economic Concept

Market failure is an economic term that describes a situation when market outcomes make society worse off. Market failure happens when companies focus, as they should, on profitable activities, but these profitable activities do not maximize the public good and may even harm the public. Typically, market failure is caused by unpriced externalities.

Externalities are side effects or consequences of activities that impact parties outside the activities but are not included in the price of goods or services in the activity.

The outside party impacted by an externality is often the public. Positive externalities increase public good, and negative externalities decrease public good.

# Electricity Sector

Market failure in the electricity sector explains why some operating nuclear power plants are being closed early due to financial losses and why some countries are building new nuclear power plants, and other countries are not.

In the electricity industry, combustion-based electricity is cheap, due in part to unpriced negative externalities. Combustion-based power plants can dump carbon dioxide and other combustion wastes into the environment with no cost and few limits. The public bears the cost of this negative externality in global warming and in health problems from breathing air emissions. Air emissions public costs are not reflected in combustion fuel prices, combustion-based power plant costs, or electricity spot market prices. Fossil fuel air emissions are a clear example of an unpriced negative externality.

In the new approach to the electricity industry, commodity wholesale electricity prices are the basis for power plant investment and operation decisions. Low electricity market prices caused by low-cost combustion-based electricity (i.e., a direct result of the unpriced negative externality of air emissions) result in a lower value for nuclear electricity.

# Nuclear Power

Nuclear power plants provide clean electricity and other public benefits with little or no compensation. These are examples of unpriced positive externalities.

The combination of unpriced negative externalities from combustion-based generation air emissions and uncompensated positive externalities for nuclear power plants results in market failure. This market failure is seen when electricity markets provide incentives for more combustion-based power plants, but existing nuclear power plants are closed early, and new nuclear power plants are not developed.[58]

This market failure lowers the public good for society.

# Market Failure

# NUCLEAR POWER IN THE REAL WORLD

*"With nuclear power facing an uncertain future in many countries, the world risks a steep decline in its use in advanced economies that could result in billions of tonnes of additional carbon emissions. Some countries have opted out of nuclear power in light of concerns about safety and other issues. Many others, however, still see a role for nuclear in their energy transitions but are not doing enough to meet their goals."*

International Energy Agency - *Nuclear Power in a Clean Energy System*[59]

More than half of the world's nuclear power capacity is in five countries, the US, the UK, Canada, France, and China. These countries have different electricity industry approaches that have shaped and continue to shape each country's nuclear power industry.

This chapter looks at nuclear power in the world and each of these five countries. Nuclear power is linked to the electricity industry approach in these countries, and examining the issues in these countries shows market failure related to nuclear power.

# World

> *"Securing continued generation from the approximately 290 reactors which have been operating for more than 30 years, and which have the potential to generate for decades to come, is the cheapest way to generate low-carbon electricity."*
>
> World Nuclear Association - *World Nuclear Performance Report 2020*[60]

Most of the world's nuclear power capacity, shown in Figure 9, was built and placed into commercial operation between 1970 and 2000. Between 2000 and 2020, slightly more nuclear power plant capacity was added than was closed.

Figure 9 shows nuclear power capacity data, in MWe, for 1970 - 2000 and 2000 – 2020:

- At the start and end of each period (gray bars);
- Added during the period (blue bars);
- Closed during the period (red bars); and
- Changes, mostly increases in output, during the period (green bars).

The same graphical approach used in Figure 9 is used to present nuclear power capacity for each of the countries examined.

## Figure 9 - World Nuclear Capacity

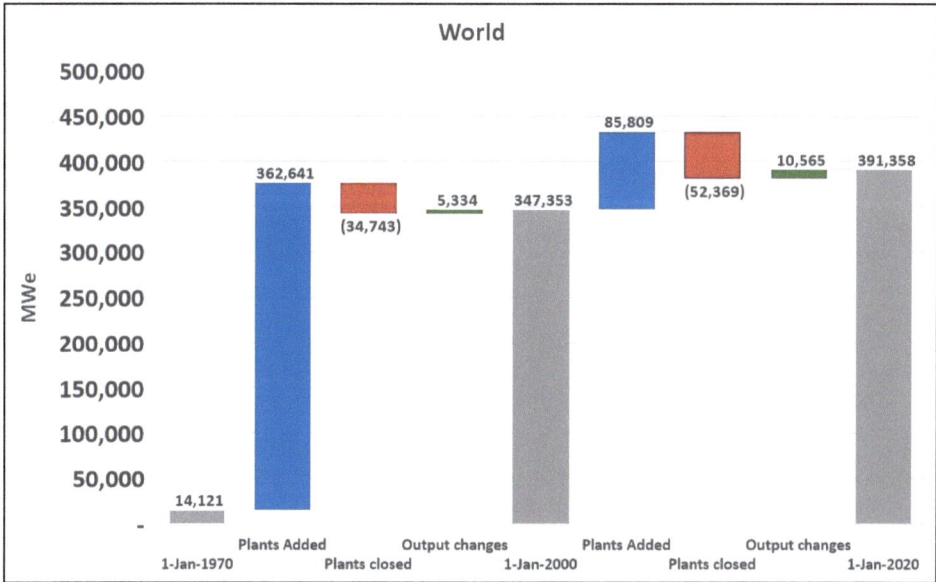

*Source: International Atomic Energy Agency Power Reactor Information System data, with analysis by the author.*

World nuclear power capacity outcomes hide different situations at the country level. A detailed discussion of nuclear power capacity for the US, the UK, Canada, France, and China follows.

# US

*"The U.S. approach ... will likely result in more nuclear power units retiring early to stop additional financial losses to merchant nuclear power plant owners."*

Idaho National Laboratory - *Economic and Market Challenges Facing the U.S. Nuclear Commercial Fleet – Cost and Revenue Study*[61]

The US has the largest nuclear power fleet in the world. The US also has a unique electricity industry, with the traditional electricity industry approach in some regions and the new electricity industry approach (i.e., a restructured and deregulated electricity sector with an electricity market) in other regions.

Traditional regulated electric utilities developed all US nuclear power plants in operation and are building the only new nuclear power plant under construction in 2020.

In the regions with the new electricity industry approach, nuclear power plants are closing, and no new nuclear power plants are being built.

### Nuclear power

Figure 10 shows US nuclear power capacity.

Most US nuclear power plants were built between 1970 and 2000. New nuclear power plant capacity added after 2000 was from the completion or restart of two plants (Browns Ferry 2 and Watts Bar 2) that started construction in the 1970s. Only one new nuclear project, the Vogtle expansion project, was under construction in 2020.

The US nuclear power plant fleet is shrinking. Since 1970, more than 19,000 MWe of nuclear power capacity was closed. 6,778 MWe of nuclear power capacity closed between 1 January 2013 and 1 January 2020, with another 1,599 MWe closing in 2020. An additional 8,164 MWe of nuclear power capacity is scheduled to close by 2025. Even more nuclear power plants face financial stress and potential closure.[62]

All US nuclear power plants in operation were built by traditional regulated or government electric utilities, and a traditional regulated electric utility was building the only new nuclear power plant under construction in 2020. Private, shareholder-owned nuclear industrial companies (e.g., General Electric and Westinghouse) sold and built these nuclear power plants. The shareholder-owned US nuclear industrial sector is different from the government-owned nuclear industrial companies in China, France, Russia, and other countries.

## Figure 10 - Nuclear Capacity in the US

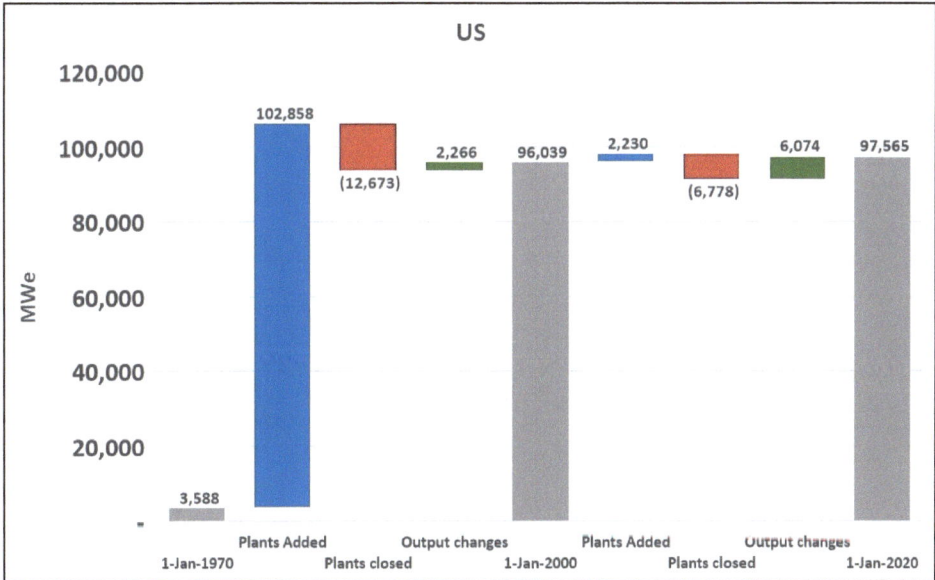

Source: *International Atomic Energy Agency Power Reactor Information System data, with analysis by the author.*

## *US Electricity Reform*

For almost a century, the US electricity system was dominated by vertically-integrated electric utilities subject to economic regulation.

Starting in about 1990, some US states and regions moved to the new electricity industry approach (i.e., a privatized and deregulated electricity industry with electricity markets). US states have oversight of regulated electric utilities and decide on electricity industry deregulation and restructuring. The US federal government oversees wholesale electricity sales and electricity markets. This mix of state and federal oversight of the US electricity industry is complicated. The move to reform the US electricity sector increased the role of the federal government.

## *Electricity markets*

The US Federal Energy Regulatory Commission (FERC) oversees wholesale electricity. The FERC oversight of wholesale electricity includes the review and approval of US electricity markets shown in Figure 11.

## Figure 11 - US Electricity Markets

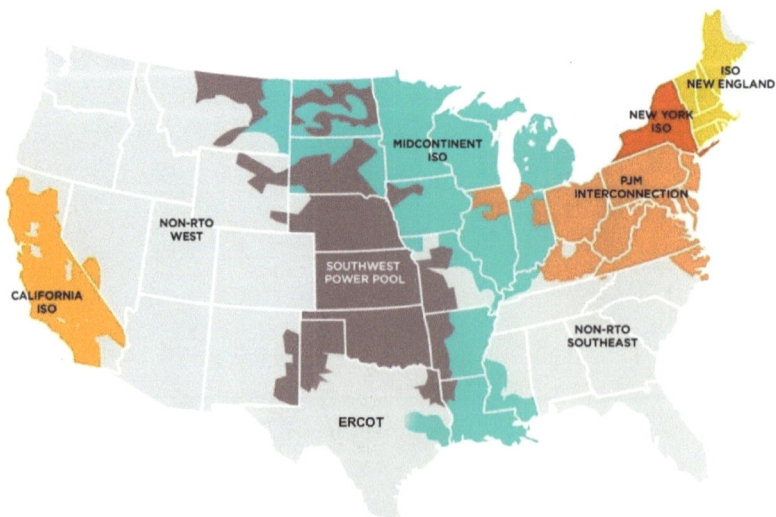

*Source: US Federal Energy Regulatory Commission*

These electricity markets are similar but not identical, with each having independent transmission system and market operators

Some of these electricity markets started as power pools, where multiple regulated utilities participated in joint dispatch, generation planning, and other activities. The Pennsylvania-New Jersey-Maryland Interconnection (PJM), New England, and New York power pools evolved into the new PJM, ISO-NE, and NYISO electricity markets.

Texas and California created the new Electric Reliability Council of Texas (ERCOT) and California Independent System Operator (CAISO) electricity markets.

Some US regions created new regional electricity markets, including the Midcontinent Independent System Operator (MISO) and Southwest Power Pool (SPP) markets.

### State-level deregulation

In addition to developing wholesale electricity markets, the US electricity reform process included state implementation of electricity industry deregulation and restructuring.

Some states decided that they would not implement electricity reform. The southeast and west outside California (i.e., the white areas in Figure 11) regions retain the traditional electricity industry structure and are outside the electricity markets. However, wholesale electricity is not constrained by state or electricity market borders, so regions with a traditional electricity approach are influenced by electricity markets in neighboring regions.

Other states restructured vertically-integrated utilities, with important differences in how this was done.

In some states, regulated utilities were required to divest all electricity generation assets, including nuclear power plants. These divested power plants were purchased by non-regulated generation companies, creating new merchant power plants that would participate in newly established wholesale electricity markets.

In other states, regulated utilities could shift their electricity generation assets into new unregulated subsidiaries (i.e., rather than divesting the assets). The power plants owned and operated by these unregulated generation subsidiaries act as merchant generators that participate in wholesale electricity markets.

A few states allowed vertically-integrated utilities to retain regulated power plants that participate in a wholesale electricity market but remain state-regulated utility assets.

### Merchant Nuclear Plants

US electricity industry deregulation and restructuring created a new class of merchant power plants in the early 2000s, some of which were nuclear power plants.

The divestment and purchase of merchant nuclear power plants usually included a transition PPA. In these PPAs, the original nuclear power plant owner buys power from the new owner, insulating both parties from direct financial exposure to electricity market prices. These nuclear power PPAs typically expired when the nuclear power plant's original 40-year NRC operating license expired (i.e., a term of about ten years). When these PPAs expired, merchant nuclear power plants had direct financial exposure to electricity market prices.

The buyers of merchant nuclear power plants were mostly utility companies with one or more nuclear power plants. The buyer would add the acquired merchant nuclear power plant to its existing nuclear power fleet, then undertake work to bring the newly acquired merchant nuclear power plant up to its existing nuclear fleet's cost and performance levels. The new owner would also request NRC approval to operate the acquired nuclear power plant for 20 years after the original NRC operating license expiry. An approved license renewal application would add 20 years of operating life after the transitional PPA ends.

A typical merchant nuclear power plant business plan assumed that electricity market prices, and the value of nuclear electricity, would increase during the transitional PPA term. After the transitional PPA expired, higher electricity market prices would provide the merchant nuclear project with increased revenue from a new PPA or sales into the electricity market. This higher revenue would provide a return on the investment made to buy the merchant nuclear power plant, improve plant performance, and obtain NRC license renewal approval.

Most merchant nuclear power plants faced lower, not higher, electricity market prices at the end of transitional PPAs. Lower electricity market prices were due to a combination of low natural gas prices (i.e., due to US shale gas production), low demand growth (i.e., due to a shift away from traditional manufacturing in the US), and investments in renewable energy projects (i.e., due to state and federal incentives).

Low electricity market prices led to the cancellation or indefinite postponement of all planned new merchant nuclear power projects, financial losses by existing merchant nuclear power plants after transitional PPAs expired, and the closure of multiple merchant nuclear power plants facing financial losses.

### Nuclear Renaissance

The creation of US merchant nuclear power plants took place when a wave of new nuclear power plants, referred to as the nuclear renaissance, was expected to happen.

The nuclear renaissance was driven by some of the same expectations behind the merchant nuclear power model, including projections that electricity demand would grow and fossil fuel prices would increase. There were also expectations that climate change concerns would become more urgent and increase the value of clean nuclear electricity, and that the cost and time to build new nuclear power plants would be lower due to new designs and construction techniques.

In this period, the new Part 52 NRC licensing approach for nuclear power plants was implemented. This new licensing approach removed a key risk in the earlier NRC licensing approach. Part 52 allowed a new nuclear project to obtain a combined construction and operation license (COL) before making an investment decision and starting construction. In the earlier Part 50 NRC approach, a nuclear power project went through a review and hearing process to obtain a construction license, but a second review and hearing process was required to obtain an operating license after the nuclear power plant was built.

The US implemented the Energy Policy Act of 2005 that provided multiple incentives for new US nuclear power projects, including loan guarantees, production tax credits, and regulatory risk insurance.[63]

By 2008, dozens of new US nuclear power projects were announced, and multiple COL applications were filed with the NRC. Some of these new nuclear power projects would be merchant power plants.

Later, as it became clear that electricity market prices and other assumptions did not support new nuclear power plant investments, most of these new nuclear power projects were put on hold, indefinitely postponed, or abandoned.

### New Nuclear Power Projects

Only two projects from the nuclear renaissance period started construction, Vogtle 3 & 4 in Georgia and V.C. Summer 2 & 3 in South Carolina. Both projects are regulated power plants under the traditional electricity industry approach, with added incentives from state laws and regulations to encourage new nuclear power investment. The V.C. Summer 2 & 3 project started construction but was abandoned in 2017. The Vogtle 3 & 4 project is still under construction.

In 2020, other US new nuclear power projects were under development, including the NuScale Utah Associated Municipal Power Systems (UAMPS) project in Idaho. The US federal government is providing targeted support for R&D related to new SMR and advanced reactor projects.

### Early Closures Before 2000

The US nuclear power plants that closed before 2000 were mostly Gen I units that had reached the end of their useful life. Several Gen II units were closed due to accidents (i.e., Three Mile Island Unit 2 and Rancho Seco), major maintenance issues (e.g., Trojan and Zion units 1 and 2), or regulatory issues (i.e., Shoreham).

The Trojan[64] and Zion[65] PWR nuclear power plants were closed because of problems with steam generator corrosion. Many PWR units operating today faced similar steam generator corrosion issues but replaced their original steam generators to address these issues.

Before 2000, electricity markets were not a direct issue in US nuclear power plant early closures. However, if the full value of nuclear electricity had been recognized and compensated, some of these early closures may not have happened. This higher value for nuclear electricity would provide a financial incentive to invest in major maintenance needed for these nuclear power plants to continue operation.

### *Early Closures After 2012*

6,778 MWe of US nuclear power capacity was closed between 2000 and 2020, as shown in Figure 10, and two plants (i.e., 601 MWe Duane Arnold and 998 MWe Indian Point-2) were closed in 2020 after the period covered in Figure 10. These closures, shown in Figure 12, provide several examples of nuclear power market failure.

## Figure 12 - US recent nuclear power plant closures

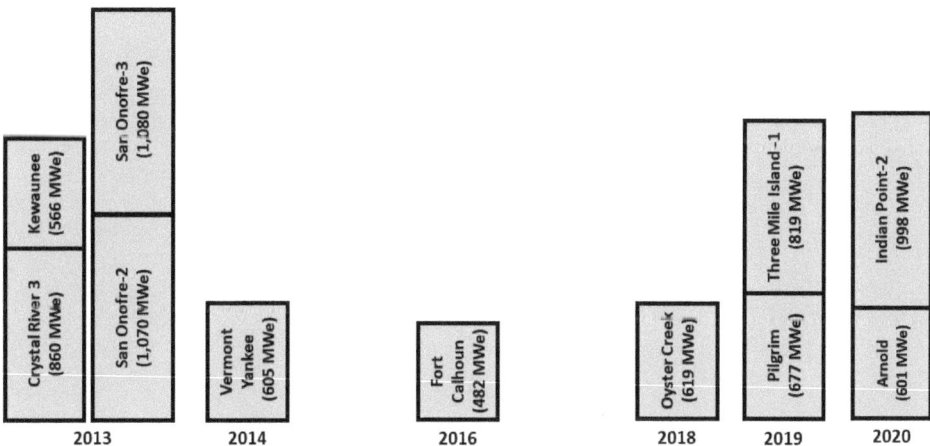

These nuclear power plant closures are discussed below.

### Crystal River and San Onofre

The Crystal River and San Onofre nuclear power plants were closed early for major maintenance issues.  A higher value for nuclear electricity might have prevented the closure of these nuclear power plants.  Both these nuclear power plants were assets of investor-owned regulated utilities.

Even if the cost of repairing an existing nuclear power plant is high, repairing a nuclear power plant and returning it to commercial operation may involve lower cost and lower risk compared to building a new nuclear power plant.  If the existing nuclear power plant's continued operation is profitable, the economic case for repairing an existing nuclear power plant and operating for 80 years or longer is compelling.

Crystal River 3 is an 860 MWe PWR owned and operated by a regulated utility.  The plant started operation in 1976.  Steam generators were replaced at Crystal River 3 in 2009, but the replacement project damaged the reactor containment structure.  The unit did not operate after 2009 and was closed in 2013.

San Onofre 2 and 3 are 1,070 and 1.080 MWe PWRs owned by regulated and public power utilities in California.  The units started operation in 1983 and 1984.  Steam generators were replaced in both San Onofre units, but the new replacement steam generators had issues that led the owner to close the units in 2013.[66]

### Kewaunee

The Kewaunee nuclear power plant is a 574 MWe PWR owned and operated by regulated utilities in Wisconsin.  The plant started operation in 1973.

In 2005, the Kewaunee nuclear power plant was sold to Dominion Resources as a merchant nuclear power plant.  The sale included a PPA that expired in December 2013.

The Dominion Resources plan was to invest in the plant to reduce costs, increase reliability, increase output levels, and increase operating life. The expectation was that the value of nuclear electricity would increase over time, making this a profitable long-term investment.

After the purchase, Dominion Resources applied for and received approval from the NRC to operate Kewaunee until 2033.

As the PPA neared the end of its term, Dominion Resources could not find a replacement PPA and would be forced to sell Kewaunee's output into short-term electricity markets at very low prices. Faced with the prospect of operating the plant at a financial loss, Dominion Resources closed the plant on 7 May 2013.[67]

### Vermont Yankee

Vermont Yankee was a 605 MWe BWR in Vermont that started operation in 1972. Vermont Yankee was owned and operated by the Vermont Yankee Nuclear Power Corporation (VYNPC; a nuclear operating company owned by eight regional regulated electric utilities).

In 2002, Vermont Yankee was sold to Entergy and became Entergy Nuclear Vermont Yankee. The acquisition included a 10-year PPA with three of the original owners.

Entergy's business plan was to invest in the plant to reduce costs, increase reliability, increase output levels, and increase operating life. The expectation was that the value of nuclear electricity would increase over time, making this a profitable long-term investment.

After purchasing Vermont Yankee, Entergy received NRC approval to implement a 120% power uprate in 2006 and applied for a 20-year NRC operating license renewal.

Entergy sought new power contracts to replace the PPAs that were part of the Vermont Yankee purchase. No new PPAs were available because wholesale electricity market prices were lower than Vermont Yankee generating costs, and there was uncertainty about the continued operation of Vermont Yankee after March 2012 (i.e., when the original NRC operating license expired). Uncertainty about Vermont Yankee's future operation was due to Vermont state government opposition to Entergy's license renewal application to the NRC. Entergy prevailed in court and received NRC approval to operate for an additional 20 years, until March 2032.

However, with no new power contracts, Vermont Yankee faced losses in the wholesale electricity market and was closed in December 2014.

### Fort Calhoun

The Fort Calhoun Nuclear Generating Station is a 482 MWe PWR owned by the Omaha Public Power District (OPPD), a public power utility in Nebraska. The plant started operation in 1973.

In 2003, Fort Calhoun received approval to operate an additional twenty years, until August 2033. The Fort Calhoun plant was refurbished in 2006, replacing steam generators, pressurizer, reactor vessel head, low-pressure turbines, and main transformer.

Fort Calhoun was a regulated asset of OPPD, which was a member of the SPP electricity market. Nebraska and nearby Iowa have extensive wind generation and low electricity prices. Fort Calhoun was a smaller single-unit nuclear power plant with generating costs that were higher than US averages.

Electricity generated by Fort Calhoun was more expensive than electricity from other sources available to OPPD. OPPD closed the plant in 2016 to reduce customer rates, despite having approval to operate the plant until 2033.

### Oyster Creek

The Oyster Creek Nuclear Generating Station is a 619 MWe BWR owned and operated by a regulated utility in New Jersey. The plant started operation in 1969.

In 1999, Oyster Creek was sold to AmerGen, now Exelon, with the sale including a PPA

The NRC approved a 20-year license renewal allowing the plant to operate until 2029. In 2010, an agreement was reached between Exelon and the state of New Jersey to close the plant in 2019, ten years early, to avoid a requirement to retrofit a cooling tower to replace the direct cooling system.

Exelon closed Oyster Creek on 17 September 2018, even earlier than planned, due to low electricity market prices.[68]

### Pilgrim

The Pilgrim Nuclear Power Station (Pilgrim) is a 677 MWe BWR owned and operated by a regulated utility. The plant started operation in 1972.

In 1999, Pilgrim was sold to Entergy, with PPAs covering 22% of its output.

The NRC approved a 20-year license renewal allowing operation until 2032, after a six-year review process.[69] Despite having the approval to operate until 2032, Entergy closed the Pilgrim nuclear power plant in May 2019 due to low wholesale electricity market prices.

### Three Mile Island Unit 1

The Three Mile Island Generating Station Unit 1 (TMI-1) is an 819 MWe PWR owned and operated by a regulated utility in Pennsylvania. The unit started operation in 1974.

In 1998, TMI-1 was purchased by AmerGen Energy, now Exelon.

The NRC approved a 20-year license renewal allowing operation until 2034.

Exelon announced that it was experiencing financial losses at TMI-1 as early as 2015 and that the plant would be closed unless Pennsylvania took action that would provide the plant with additional revenue.

TMI Unit 1 was closed on 20 September 2019 due to low electricity market prices.

### Duane Arnold

The Duane Arnold nuclear power plant is a 601 MWe BWR owned and operated by a consortium of regulated and public power utilities in Iowa. The plant started operation in 1975.

In 2006, FPL Energy, now NextEra Energy, bought the 70% share of the plant held by Alliant Energy. The sale was accompanied by a PPA that expired in February 2014, when the original NRC operating license was to expire.

In 2010, the NRC approved a 20-year license extension that allowed operation until 2034.

In 2013, the Iowa Utilities Board allowed the parties to amend and extend the PPA by about 12 years.

The parties agreed to terminate the amended PPA five years early (i.e., in 2020) due to low electricity market prices in return for a $110 million buyout payment from Alliant.[70]

NextEra announced that they would close the Duane Arnold nuclear power plant in October 2020 at the end of the PPA, but the plant was closed even earlier, in August 2020, after a windstorm damaged the plant's cooling towers.

### *Scheduled Early Closures*

Another 8,164 MWe of US nuclear power capacity is scheduled to close by 2025, as shown in Figure 13.

## Figure 13 - Scheduled US early nuclear power plant closures

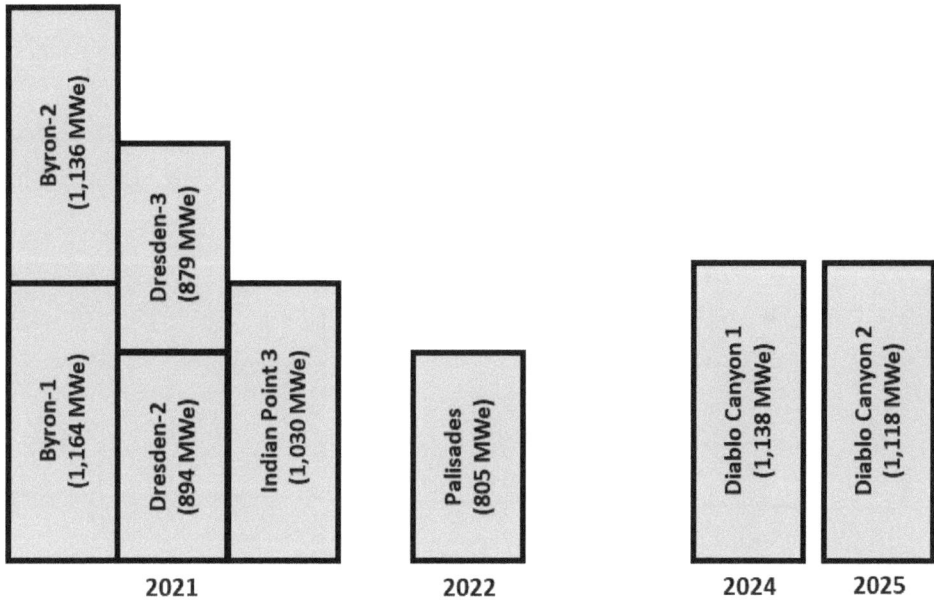

These scheduled closures are for multiple reasons, as discussed below.

### *Byron and Dresden*

The Byron nuclear power plant has two PWR units, 1,164 and 1,136 MWe, owned and operated by a regulated utility in Illinois. The units started operation in 1985 and 1987. Both units have received approval for 20-year license renewal, with NRC operating license valid until 2044 and 2046.

The Dresden nuclear power plant has two BWR units, 894 and 879 MWe, owned and operated by a regulated utility in Illinois. The units started operation in 1970 and 1971. Both units have received approval for 20-year license renewal, with NRC operating license valid until 2029 and 2031.

In 1997, Illinois electricity sector reform required that the owner of these two plants, Commonwealth Edison, transfer ownership of the plants to an unregulated affiliate, Exelon Generation. The Illinois deregulation process involved power contracts for these plants that have expired, and the plants now rely on sales into the electricity market for revenue.

In August 2020, Exelon announced that it would close the Byron and Dresden plants in 2021 due to low electricity market prices.[71]

### *Palisades*

The Palisades nuclear power plant is a 725 MWe PWR owned and operated by a regulated utility in Michigan. The plant started operation in 1973.

Palisades was sold to Entergy in 2007, along with a PPA that ends in 2022.

The NRC approved a 20-year license renewal to operate the Palisades nuclear power plant until 2031.

Palisade PPA prices are higher than electricity market prices, leading to a negotiated agreement in 2018 to terminate the PPA early, with a Consumers Energy payment to Entergy (i.e., a buy-out of the above-market contract). The Michigan Public Service Commission rejected the PPA early termination agreement.

The Palisades plant continues to operate and sell power to Consumers Energy. Entergy will close the plant when the PPA expires in 2022.

### *Indian Point 2 and 3*

The Indian Point plant has three nuclear power units. Indian Point 1 was a 275 MWe PWR that started operation in 1962 and was closed in 1974. The Indian Point 2 and 3 PWR units, 998 and 1,030 MWe, started operation in 1974 and 1976. Both units were owned by Consolidated Edison, a regulated investor-owned utility. Indian Point 3 was sold to the New York Power Authority (NYPA), a public power utility, in 1976.

Entergy purchased the Indian Point nuclear units in 2000 (Indian Point 3) and 2001 (Indian Point 1 and 2). The purchases included PPAs, which expired by 2009.

The original NRC operating licenses expired in September 2013 for Indian Point 2 and in December 2015 for Indian Point 3. Entergy applied to the NRC for 20-year license renewals for both units in 2007, but litigation opposing the application was filed. This litigation called for Indian Point to replace its direct water cooling with a new closed-cycle cooling tower system.

The litigation delayed NRC approval past the original operation license expiration dates, but Indian Point continued to operate under an NRC rule that allows a nuclear power plant's continued operation past its original license expiration if a timely filing of a license extension application was made.

Electricity market prices in the NYISO market near New York City, where the Indian Point nuclear power plant is located, are relatively high, and Indian Point is not reported to be experiencing financial losses.

After more than a decade of litigation, Entergy and New York state reached an agreement to settle the Indian Point litigation in 2017. The settlement includes closing the Indian Point units in 2020 and 2021.

### Diablo Canyon 1 and 2

The Diablo Canyon nuclear power plant has 1,138 MWe and 1,118 MWe PWR units owned and operated by Pacific Gas & Electric (PG&E), a regulated utility in California. The Diablo Canyon units started operation in 1985 and 1986, and their original 40-year operating licenses expire in November 2024 and August 2025.

The California state electricity reform process allowed PG&E to retain the Diablo Canyon nuclear power plant as a regulated utility asset that operates in the CAISO electricity market.

PG&E filed an application with the NRC for a 20-year license renewal for the Diablo Canyon units in November 2009.

In June 2016, before the license renewal applications were approved, PG&E announced a Joint Proposal with environmental organizations and other parties to phase out nuclear power and increase energy efficiency, renewables, and electricity storage investments.[72]

The Joint Proposal included closing Diablo Canyon Units 1 and 2 when their original operating licenses expire in 2024 and 2025. PG&E's application to close Diablo Canyon was approved by the California Public Utilities Commission in 2018, after which PG&E withdrew the Diablo Canyon license renewal application.

### *Early Closure Avoided by State Actions*

Some US nuclear power plants with poor financial performance in electricity markets remained in operation due to action taken by US states. These states increased revenue to threatened merchant nuclear power plants by establishing Zero Emissions Credit (ZEC) programs, by allowing nuclear power to participate in clean energy auctions, and by joining regional emissions initiatives.

The nuclear power plants that continue to operate due to ZEC payments include Ginna, FitzPatrick, and Nine Mile Point in New York; Quad Cities and Clinton in Illinois; Hope Creek and Salem in New Jersey; and Davis-Besse and Perry in Ohio.

The Millstone nuclear power plant remained in operation due to additional revenue from a power contract awarded in a clean energy auction process in Connecticut.

ZEC programs were considered in Pennsylvania but were not adopted, leading to the early closure of Three Mile Island 1 in 2020. Pennsylvania's plans to join the Regional Greenhouse Gas Initiative (RGGI), a program for capping and gradually decreasing carbon dioxide emissions from the power sector in 10 Northeast and Mid-Atlantic states, was a factor in keeping the Beaver Valley nuclear power plant from closing early in 2021.

### *Threatened Nuclear Power Plants*

In 2020, other nuclear power plants in several US states face financial pressure from low electricity market prices, and these nuclear power plants are at risk of early closure unless state support is provided.

### *Illinois*

Exelon announced that the two twin-unit LaSalle and Braidwood nuclear power plants in Illinois are at risk of early closure. [73]

Illinois may take action to provide ZEC payments to some of these nuclear power plants in time to prevent early closure. Illinois has also considered a plan to leave the PJM capacity market due to new federal rules related to the capacity market auction. [74]

### *Pennsylvania*

Pennsylvania declined to put a ZEC program in place, resulting in the early closure of Three Mile Island Unit 1 in 2019. The twin unit Beaver Valley nuclear power plant, owned by Energy Harbor Nuclear Corporation (formerly FirstEnergy), was scheduled to close early in 2021, but the owner rescinded a deactivation notice for the plant in 2020 due to Pennsylvania's decision to join RGGI. [75] It is unclear if membership in RGGI will provide enough additional revenue for the Beaver Valley plant to stop a future early closure decision. The Beaver Valley plant remains at risk of early closure.

### *Ohio*

In 2018, FirstEnergy (now Energy Harbor Nuclear Corporation) issued deactivation notices for the Davis-Besse and Perry nuclear power plants. These deactivation notices were rescinded in July 2019 because Ohio put a ZEC payment plan in place.

Ohio House Bill 6 (HB6), the legislation that established the ZEC payments in Ohio, is the focus of a corruption investigation. Several Ohio state legislators were arrested in 2020. State legislation to repeal HB 6 or stop

ZEC payments has been introduced.  If ZEC payments to Davis-Besse and Perry nuclear power plants stop, these two nuclear power plants are at risk of early closure.

### *Insights*

The US nuclear power industry, despite its size and historical success, is declining.

This decline can be directly linked to the US market approach to nuclear power and the implementation of electricity markets in regions of the US with many nuclear power plants.

Existing nuclear power plants have been closed early as a direct result of low electricity market prices.  More existing nuclear power plants are scheduled to close early in the next few years, and more existing nuclear power plants are at risk of early closure.  A market approach to nuclear power means that few new nuclear power plants will be built in the US.

The situation in parts of the US with a traditional electricity industry approach is better, but problems remain.  Few regulated nuclear power plants have closed early, but some are at risk.  While one regulated nuclear power plant is under construction, no others are currently planned, even though several have NRC approval to start construction.

The US provides a clear example of market failure for nuclear power in the new electricity market approach.  Even in US traditional electricity industry regions, the low value of electricity means no new nuclear power plants are being built.

# United Kingdom

*"Nuclear never has and cannot exist in
a private market setting."*

Molly Scott Cato - *British Member of
European Parliament*[76]

The UK was an early adopter of nuclear power and built a relatively large nuclear power fleet before 1970. The UK was also one of the first countries to move to the new market-based electricity industry approach.

### Nuclear Power

UK nuclear power plant capacity was built by the Central Electricity Generating Board (CEGB), a government-owned electric utility.

Figure 14 shows the nuclear power generation capacity in the UK.

The UK nuclear power fleet was built before 2000. Several UK nuclear power plants have closed since 2000, and all older operating nuclear power plants using Advanced Gas-cooled Reactor (AGR) technology will be closed by 2030. The UK needs new nuclear power plant capacity to replace closed nuclear power plants and meet the UK's climate change goals.

The UK has one nuclear power plant under construction, HPC, and several other nuclear power projects under development. Outside companies are building these new UK nuclear power plants as merchant generators operating in the UK electricity market, although none would proceed without substantial out-of-market financial incentives.

## Figure 14 - Nuclear Capacity in the UK

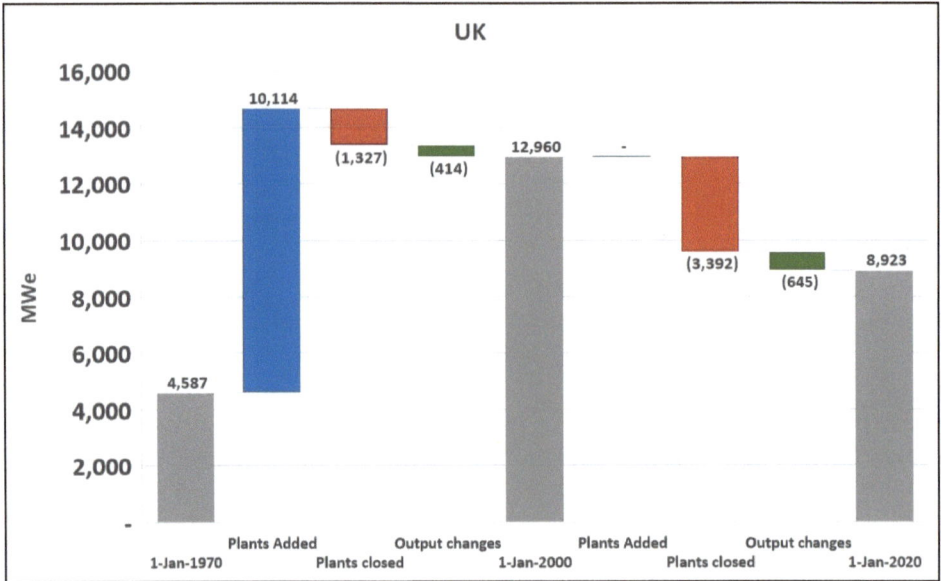

Source: International Atomic Energy Agency Power Reactor Information System data, with analysis by the author.

### UK Electricity Reform

In the late 1980s, the UK moved to privatize the electricity industry.

In 1990, the England & Wales Electricity Pool market began trading. This electricity market provided a market for the electricity generated by newly privatized UK power plants. The UK electricity market has been through several changes and has been expanded to include Scotland.

The Electricity Act of 1989 separated the CEGB into four companies, one of which was Nuclear Electric. Nuclear Electric owned all UK nuclear power plants. Nuclear Electric remained under government ownership after other UK generating companies were privatized.

1994 legislation included plans to separate Nuclear Electric into two new entities, one of which would be privatized.

The first entity was Magnox Electric, which owned nuclear power plants using the Gen 1 Magnox reactor design. The Magnox gas-cooled nuclear power plants were considered too old and too close to decommissioning to be privatized. The last operating Magnox unit, Wylfa unit 1, was closed at the end of 2015.

The other entity, British Energy, was composed of the newer UK nuclear power plants, including seven Advanced Gas Reactor (AGR) plants and the Sizewell B PWR plant.

### British Energy

British Energy was privatized through a stock flotation on 14 July 1996, well after UK non-nuclear power plants were privatized. After privatization, British Energy experienced financial problems as a merchant generator in the UK electricity market. The UK government re-nationalized British Energy in 2005.[77]

British Energy was sold to EDF in 2009 and became part of EDF Energy. EDF Energy is a major participant in the UK electricity sector, which had earlier acquired the London Electricity Board, other electricity boards, and power plants.

EDF Energy is a subsidiary of EDF, the French government-owned utility and nuclear power plant owner. The purchase of British Energy was made, in part, to obtain existing nuclear power sites that would be potential sites for new nuclear power plants. The UK government had committed to aggressive carbon reduction goals that were only achievable if new nuclear power plants were built. Owning the sites of existing nuclear power plants would provide an edge for a developer who wanted to build new nuclear power plants, like EDF.

EDF Energy was required to sell some sites to other potential nuclear power plant developers to obtain competition regulator approval to acquire British Energy.

### Existing Nuclear Power Plants

EDF Energy owns and operates several aging AGR units and the Sizewell B PWR unit. The AGR units are nearing the end of their operating life, and some have closed.

Unlike the merchant nuclear plants in the US, the EDF Energy nuclear power plant fleet appears to be profitable due to a combination of relatively high electricity market revenue, capacity market revenue, EU Emissions Trading System revenue, and financial benefits of hedging EDF Energy's electricity customer sales.

### New Nuclear Program

The UK government acknowledged that new nuclear power plants were needed to replace aging AGR nuclear power plants and to meet electricity carbon emission goals. The UK also decided that new nuclear power capacity should be built as merchant power plants but acknowledged that the UK electricity market would not support new merchant nuclear power investments. These new UK merchant nuclear power projects would require substantial out-of-market incentives.[78]

A 2011 White Paper committed the UK Government to a series of reforms, referred to as Electricity Market Reform (EMR), to ensure reliable, affordable, and low-carbon electricity. EMR policy objectives were to be achieved using a capacity market, power contracts (i.e., contracts for difference, or CfDs), a carbon price floor, and emissions performance standards. The UK's EMR incentives were used to encourage merchant nuclear power plant investments.[79] The HPC project was the first nuclear power project to receive EMR incentives.

### HPC, Sizewell C, and Bradwell

The HPC nuclear project was the first new UK nuclear power plant since Sizewell B, a PWR project that started operation in 1995. The HPC project is a merchant nuclear power plant that will operate in the UK electricity market and was the first merchant power plant to move forward under EMR incentives and HPC is now under construction.[80]  The HPC project is linked to a second EPR nuclear power plant at Sizewell C.

HPC owner motives go beyond financial returns, with the HPC project achieving strategic and geopolitical objectives of the foreign national nuclear owners, EDF Energy and CGN.

The HPC project should demonstrate that the French EPR technology is feasible, despite the serious cost and schedule issues at the Finnish Olkiluoto 3 EPR project and the French Flamanville 3 EPR project.  Success at HPC would help sell the EPR technology in other countries and lower the risks of building more nuclear power plants in France using EPR technology through learning during the HPC and Sizewell C projects.  The HPC and Sizewell C projects will also help maintain French nuclear industrial capability and nuclear power industry jobs in France.

CGN's investment in HPC builds on the success of the Chinese EPR nuclear power plants at Taishan, built by Chinese companies using the French EPR design.  CGN's HPC investment was conditional on UK government approval of a new nuclear power plant project at the Bradwell site built and owned by Chinese companies that would use the Chinese Hualong One reactor technology.  The Hualong One reactor design is the primary Chinese reactor design offered for export.  Having the Hualong One reactor design approved by the UK nuclear safety regulator and built at the Bradwell site in the UK would be a strong selling point in marketing this reactor design in other countries.

### *Horizon & NuGen*

Other proposed new UK nuclear projects (e.g., Horizon and NuGeneration) were also offered an incentive package using the EMR policy mechanisms, but these two projects failed to proceed.

These two projects involved private nuclear industrial companies, Hitachi/GE, and Toshiba/Westinghouse, which saw the UK merchant nuclear projects as an opportunity to build new nuclear power plants using their Gen III ABWR and AP-1000 reactor technologies.

Like EDF Energy and CGN, the sponsors of Horizon and NuGeneration planned to use a UK merchant nuclear power plant project as a way to maintain and build their industrial capability and supply chain. Having ABWR and AP-1000 nuclear power plants approved by the UK nuclear safety regulator and built in the UK would help market these reactor designs in other countries and help lower completion risk in subsequent units due to learning.

Unlike the state-owned EDF Energy and CGN, the developers of Horizon and NuGen were private companies requiring shareholder approval to take nuclear power project completion risk. Also, the developers of the Horizon and NuGeneration projects were not owners and operators of nuclear power plants and faced a difficult transformation from nuclear industrial companies into nuclear power plant developers, owners, and operators.

### *UK Government Investment in new nuclear*

In late 2020, the UK government announced that it was considering making equity investments in new nuclear power plants. A potential equity investment in the now-abandoned Horizon project was considered in 2019 but did not happen.[81]

In the RAB Consultation Document and Energy White Paper, both released in December 2020, there are multiple mentions of the potential for UK government finance for new nuclear power plants during construction.

### *RAB*

The UK government is considering a new Regulated Asset Base (RAB) model to help developers and investors manage completion and revenue risk for new UK nuclear power plant investments.[82]

The RAB model may help convince additional merchant nuclear power plant developers to move forward. The RAB model may be used for the Sizewell C project, a copy of the HPC project. With or without the RAB scheme, the UK faces the potential of having a nuclear power sector owned and controlled by foreign state-owned nuclear power companies.

On 14 December 2020, the UK government released a summary of input received in response to the July 2019 consultation on a RAB model for new nuclear projects.[83] The government response to this input was that the RAB model is a credible approach to financing new large nuclear power plants. The UK government will explore a range of options with new nuclear power plant developers, including a RAB model and government finance during construction.

### 2020 Energy White Paper

On 14 December 2020, the UK government released the Energy White Paper, Powering our Net Zero Future.[84] This White Paper mentions nuclear power multiple times, both as a part of the current low carbon mix and as one of several technologies that will help decarbonize the UK energy system by 2050.

Nuclear power is included as one component of the Prime Minister's Ten Point Plan outlined in the Energy White Paper. A key commitment is to bring at least one large nuclear power plant project to a Financial Investment Decision before the end of the current parliament (i.e., before December 2024). The government will invest in an energy innovation programme that includes small modular and advanced modular reactors.

The White Paper refers to the RAB consultation paper released on the same day and suggests a role for UK government finance during construction.

### Insights

The UK needs new nuclear capacity and has undertaken a process to incentivize merchant nuclear power plant developers to build this capacity. The HPC arrangement was successful, and the HPC project is under construction. However, the HPC approach did not work for Horizon and NuGen. EDF Energy has also indicated that the HPC approach may not work for the Sizewell C project.

The proposed RAB approach may provide sufficient incentives to get some of these new nuclear projects to move forward. However, a more direct

Market Failure

UK Government role, including equity investments, may be needed to deliver the new UK nuclear capacity needed to meet long-term goals.

# Canada

*"Ontario has made nuclear electricity a
key element in its Long-Term Energy
Plan (LTEP) because it provides many
benefits. Low-cost electricity, clean air
and local jobs are just some of them."*

Organization of Canadian Nuclear Industries[85]

Canada has an active nuclear power program, with Canadian nuclear power plants based on the CANDU (i.e., CANadian Deuterium Uranium) PHWR technology and built by a Canadian Crown Company, Atomic Energy of Canada Limited (AECL). CANDU nuclear power plants use heavy water as a moderator and use natural (i.e., not enriched) uranium as fuel.

Most of Canada's operational nuclear power plants, as shown in Figure 15, are in Ontario, with one nuclear power plant in New Brunswick. Nuclear power provides about 50% of Ontario's electricity.

Nuclear power plant closures before 2000 and nuclear power plant additions after 2000 in Figure 15 reflect the temporary closure and return to operation of several nuclear power plant units, as discussed in more detail in the earlier discussion of long-term nuclear flexibility. Long-term flexibility to close and mothball nuclear power plants and return them to service later is an important feature of the Canadian nuclear power program.

The remainder of this section is focused on Ontario.

## Figure 15 - Nuclear Capacity in Canada

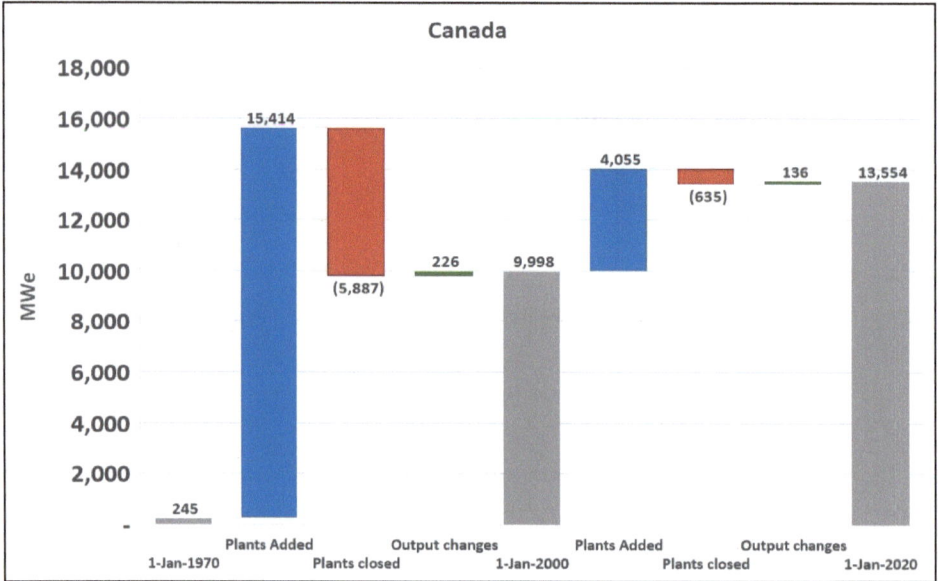

*Source: International Atomic Energy Agency Power Reactor Information System data, with analysis by the author.*

### Ontario Nuclear Power Industry

A government utility, Ontario Hydro, built the Ontario nuclear power plant fleet. In 1999, Ontario Hydro was restructured, and all power plants were transferred to Ontario Power Generation (OPG). OPG owns all nuclear power plants in Ontario, including the Bruce, Darlington, and Pickering nuclear generating stations. In 2001, Bruce Power leased the Bruce nuclear power plant from OPG, and Bruce Power is the plant's licensed operator. OPG remains the owner and operator of the Darlington and Pickering nuclear power plants.

Ontario is undertaking major capital refurbishment investments at two power plants, Bruce Power and Darlington, to extend their operating lives by an additional 30 years.

## *Ontario Electricity Industry*

The Ontario nuclear power plants operate in the Ontario electricity market system. Ontario does not rely on electricity market prices for new generation investment incentives, relying instead on government resource planning, government ownership of generation, and electricity supply contracting to manage the electricity generation mix.[86]

The Ontario electricity planning approach, laid out in its Long-Term Energy Plan, has been used to support significant nuclear power plant refurbishment investments and results in a stable and reliable electricity system with very low carbon dioxide emissions.[87]

## *Insights*

Ontario provides a different approach to fitting nuclear power into an electricity market. Rather than providing out-of-market financial incentives to nuclear power plants (e.g., US state ZEC payments and UK EMR incentives), Ontario takes a more direct role in the nuclear power sector. The Ontario government owns OPG's Darlington and Pickering nuclear power plants and has long-term contracts with Bruce Power. The government's long-term resource planning supports existing nuclear power plants and incentives for new investment (e.g., the Bruce Power and Darlington refurbishment projects).

# Market Failure

# France

*"French policy makers saw [in 1974] only one way for France to achieve energy independence: nuclear energy, a source of energy so compact that a few pounds of fissionable uranium is all the fuel needed to run a big city for a year."*

Jon Palfreman - *Why the French Like Nuclear Energy*[88]

France has the second-largest national nuclear power fleet in the world, built, owned, and operated by the French national electricity utility, EDF. EDF built about 65 GWe of capacity between 1970 and 2000, as shown in Figure 16. Nuclear power generates more than 75 percent of France's electricity needs, more than any other country.[89]

## Figure 16 - Nuclear Capacity in France

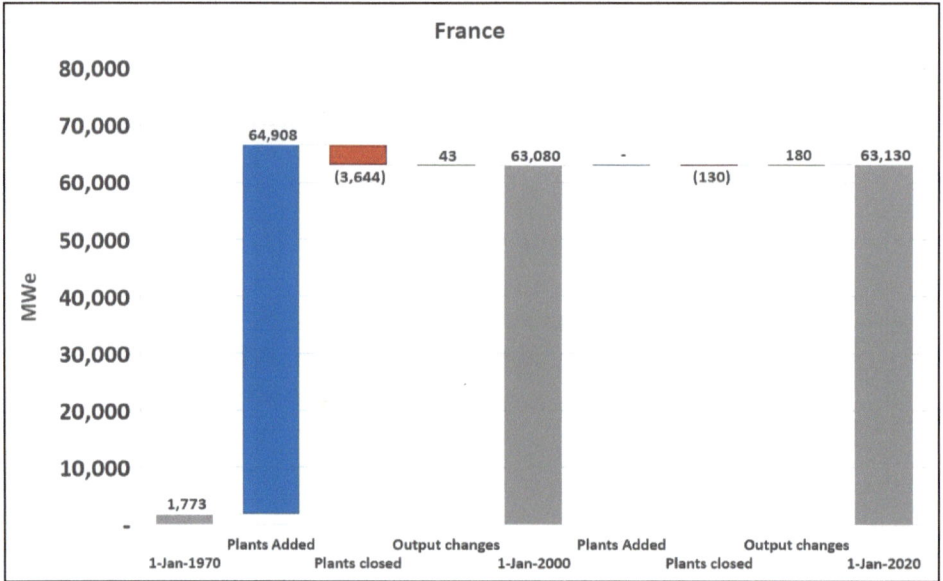

Source: International Atomic Energy Agency Power Reactor Information System
data, with analysis by the author.

The French nuclear power fleet was built by EDF with supported from other French government-owned nuclear industrial companies (e.g., Cogema and Framatome). The French nuclear power industry also built nuclear power plants in China, South Africa, South Korea, and other countries. Today, the electricity generated by French nuclear power plants is exported via high-voltage transmission lines to other European countries and via undersea transmission lines to the UK.

French government ownership of the electricity and nuclear power industries enabled the country to build a large nuclear power plant fleet to reduce France's reliance on imported fossil fuels for electricity generation. This nuclear power fleet also provides low and stable electricity prices and low carbon emissions.

The high level of nuclear generation in France limits the opportunities to build additional units, expect to replace older units that are closed. This leads to a focus on markets outside France to maintain the French nuclear industrial capability.

## *Closures*

The older Gen I nuclear power plants in France, mostly gas-cooled reactor designs, were all closed by 1994. The Super Phenix liquid metal cooled reactor was closed in 1998.

The only closure in the PWR fleet was Fessenheim. Fessenheim unit 1 closed in February 2020, and unit 2 closed in June 2020, after the period covered in Figure 16.[90] Fessenheim was the oldest operating nuclear power plant in France when it closed. The closing of Fessenheim represents a potential turning point for France. France's green growth law, passed in August 2015, limits nuclear power capacity to 63.2 GWe and requires the nuclear share of electricity generation to drop to 50 percent by 2025. The closing of Fessenheim would allow the startup of the new Flamanville 3 plant.

## *New Nuclear Projects*

One new nuclear power plant is under construction in France at the Flamanville site. Flamanville 3 uses the French EPR design used at Olkiluoto-3 in Finland, Taishan in China, and, more recently, HPC in the UK.

## *Electricity Reform*

The French nuclear power fleet was built by a traditional government-owned electric utility, with strong support from the French government. Strong government support, a capable national nuclear power industry, and assured recovery of nuclear power plant investments enabled the highly successful French nuclear build program.

The move toward electricity industry reform in France could reduce its nuclear power fleet and reduce EDF's role in the electricity sector.

## *Insights*

France is a leader in the world nuclear power industry. The success of the French nuclear power program is due, in part, to France's traditional electricity approach, a state-owned nuclear industrial sector, and government ownership of EDF and its nuclear power fleet.

# China

> *"The People's Republic of China is today the biggest platform in the world for the deployment of nuclear technology to generate electric power."*
>
> Mark Hibbs - *The Future of Nuclear Power in China*[91]

China has significant recent activity in nuclear power and the third-largest nuclear power fleet in the world. The Chinese nuclear power fleet is growing, as shown in Figure 17. In contrast to other countries, China's nuclear power fleet is relatively new.

## Figure 17 - Nuclear Capacity in China

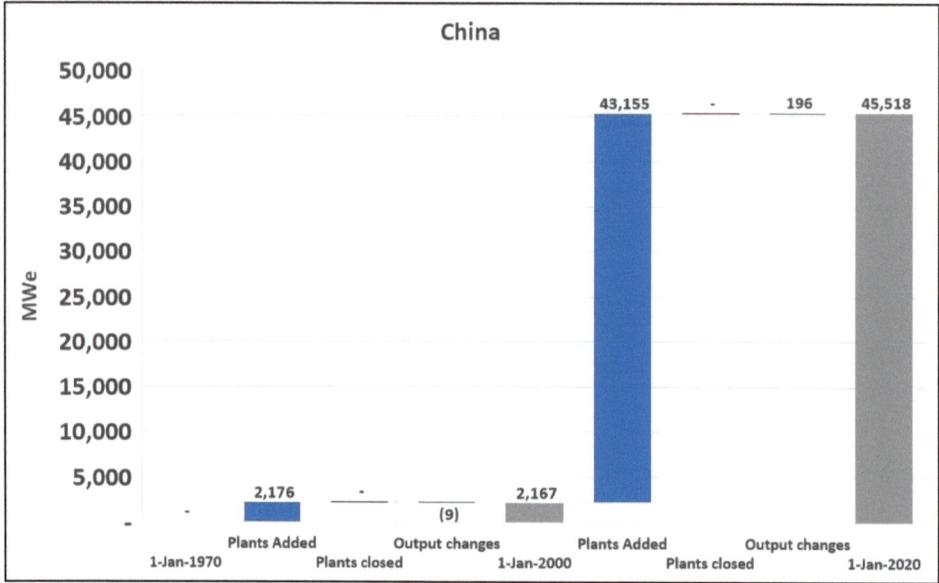

**China**

| | Plants Added | Plants closed | Output changes | Plants Added | Plants closed | Output changes | |
|---|---|---|---|---|---|---|---|
| 1-Jan-1970 | 2,176 | - | (9) | 2,167 | 43,155 | - | 196 | 45,518 |

*Source: International Atomic Energy Agency Power Reactor Information System data, with analysis by the author.*

Between 2000 and 2020, more than 43 GWe of nuclear power plant capacity was added in China. In November 2020, China had twelve nuclear power plants under construction and more nuclear power plants under development.

China has a traditional (i.e., government-owned) electricity industry and government ownership of the nuclear industrial sector. China's state-owned electricity and nuclear power industry approach, combined with clear objectives for nuclear power development, has led to a world-class nuclear power industrial capacity, a growing nuclear power plant fleet in China, and participation in the world nuclear power plant market.

The approach to nuclear power and the electricity industry in China includes a strong role of government. China is using its domestic nuclear power build program to provide much-needed clean electricity generation capacity and to develop the Chinese nuclear industrial sector. The success of the Chinese nuclear industrial sector inside China is expected to provide a strong platform for entering, and potentially dominating, the world nuclear market outside China.

# Insights

Countries with a government-owned electricity industry and a government-owned nuclear power industrial sector, like China, France, Russia, and other countries, are well-suited to develop nuclear power programs. In these countries, nuclear power can be a vital part of the electricity industry, based on national nuclear fleet and national nuclear power industrial programs.

Countries and regions with a private nuclear industrial sector and a traditional electricity industry structure may address nuclear power's challenges through utility economic regulators or national planning authorities. However, the challenges for private companies in the nuclear power sector are substantial and may lead to market failure even in the traditional electricity industry approach.

Nuclear power faces difficulty in countries or regions with the new electricity industry approach and electricity markets. Electricity markets may not provide revenue that is high enough or certain enough in the long term to keep existing nuclear power plants financially profitable or to justify new nuclear power plant investments. As seen in the US and UK, a deregulated or liberalized electricity industry may fail to support existing or new nuclear power due to market failure.

Market failure is the primary reason why nuclear power investment and activity differs across countries.

The costs of this market failure are high. Fewer nuclear power plants result in higher carbon dioxide emissions and other pollutants, less reliable base-load capacity, lower grid reliability, more volatile electricity prices, and fewer high-skilled nuclear power industry jobs. The decline in the US nuclear power industry may also result in a loss of nuclear power industry expertise and institutional knowledge.

One way to resolve nuclear power market failure is to move away from the new electricity industry approach to a government-owned electricity sector. This shift might also be linked to a government-owned nuclear power industrial sector or a substantial government role in developing new nuclear power plants.

The next chapter outlines ways to resolve nuclear power market failure.

# WHAT CAN BE DONE?

*"We have no time to experiment with visionary energy sources; civilisation is in imminent danger and has to use nuclear – the one safe, available, energy source – now or suffer the pain soon to be inflicted by our outraged planet."*

James Lovelock - *Nuclear Power is the Only Green Solution*[92]

Nuclear power is a reliable, scalable, and compact electricity source, with low or zero emissions, that provides other public goods and economic benefits.

However, electricity industry reforms, the merchant generation approach to existing and proposed nuclear power plants, private investor-owned nuclear industrial companies, and other factors are leading to market failure for nuclear power. This market failure is seen in the early closure of operating nuclear power plants and a lack of new nuclear power plants in the US and other countries.

This nuclear power market failure reduces the public good. Increasing the public good is an important role of government, and government action is needed to resolve market failure for nuclear power and deliver the public goods that nuclear power can provide.

The 2017 American Nuclear Society Toolkit has a long list of actions focused on the US market.[93]

An increased government role, a return to the traditional electricity industry approach, control of negative externalities, payment for nuclear power's positive externalities, and improved electricity market designs could help resolve nuclear power market failure.

# Increased Role of Government

> *"Even where decisions are left to the market, governments may have to intervene, as markets cannot deliver some public goods or pursue long-term goals."*
>
> OECD Nuclear Energy Agency -
> *Government and Nuclear Energy*[94]

All nuclear power plants in operation and under construction today result from direct or indirect government support. Governments can, and should, provide support for nuclear power plants that provide public benefits over 60 years or longer of operation.

Governments and regulated utilities can and do make long-term investments in public infrastructure that increase public good. Private companies, using commercial project financial analysis, are not likely to make these long-term investments in public infrastructure.

### Government-Owned Electric Utilities

Some countries already have an electricity sector that is owned by the government. Some market economies, including the US, have government utilities with nuclear power plants (e.g., the Tennessee Valley Authority) that could provide additional support for nuclear power.

Government-owned electric utilities could buy existing merchant nuclear power plants that are financially distressed, develop new nuclear power plants, and sign long-term PPAs to buy nuclear electricity from existing or new nuclear power plants.

Government-owned electric utilities that own nuclear power plants or buy nuclear electricity incur costs paid by electricity users and taxpayers, with these electricity users and taxpayers receiving the public goods these nuclear power plants provide.

New government utilities could be formed to purchase, build, own and operate nuclear power plants or to purchase the output of nuclear power plants

Governments in market economies could acquire or nationalize existing nuclear power plants to establish a state-owned nuclear power fleet. These governments could also acquire or nationalize specific nuclear power plants, as in the 2005 UK government re-nationalization of British Energy. New or existing government utilities could purchase US merchant nuclear power plants that might close early due to poor financial results.[95]

The acquisition or nationalization of all or some nuclear power plants would face significant financial, legal, political, and other issues. More targeted approaches may be more likely to succeed.

### Targeted Intervention

State or federal government intervention in the electricity industry and electricity markets could help support existing and new nuclear power.

Governments can provide higher and more certain revenue to merchant nuclear power plants than electricity spot markets by requiring government electricity users to buy nuclear electricity under long-term PPAs.

Governments might provide credit support or funding for new nuclear power projects. The US DOE loan guarantee program is an example of this. The UK announced in late 2020 that it might make equity investments in new nuclear power plants.[96]

Governments could fund nuclear power plant construction with the completed plant sold to the market after commercial operation.[97]

Government support for nuclear industrial companies could help form national nuclear power industry champions that could deliver nuclear power plants in their home country and compete with state-owned nuclear industrial companies worldwide.[98]

### Nuclear as Critical Public Infrastructure

Most countries have a direct government role in national defense, long-distance transportation (e.g., highways, railroads, airports), water, public health, and other sectors. Some countries have government-owned electricity companies, and even in countries with the new market-based electricity industry approach, the transmission system remains regulated or government-owned.

Nuclear power plant investments provide long-term public goods comparable to public goods provided by long-term infrastructure investments.

Designating nuclear power as a critical public infrastructure could be a step toward a more significant government role in supporting the nuclear power industry.

# Return to a Traditional Electricity Industry

A return to a traditional electricity industry approach could reduce the negative impact of a market approach to electricity to save existing nuclear power plants from early closure, and facilitate new nuclear power plant investments.

Existing merchant nuclear power plants could return to regulated status but continue to operate in an electricity market. There are multiple approaches to this discussed here, with examples.

### *Regulated Nuclear Power Plants in Electricity Markets*

The US states of California and Virginia allowed nuclear power plants to remain regulated utility assets even though the states moved to participate in an electricity market (i.e., CAISO in California and PJM in Virginia). Regulated nuclear power plants in California and Virginia sell electricity into the wholesale electricity market, providing utility ratepayers with a physical hedge against uncertain and volatile wholesale electricity market prices.

A merchant nuclear power plant could be returned to regulated status. An example of this was Ohio's proposal to create a new power contract between a merchant nuclear power plant and its affiliated retail electricity company.

Ohio joined the PJM electricity market and deregulated its utilities by allowing vertically-integrated utilities to transfer power plants to an unregulated subsidiary. Ohio deregulated nuclear power plants experienced low profits in the PJM electricity market and faced potential early closure.

FirstEnergy proposed that its regulated retail electricity company buy power from its unregulated nuclear power plant using a two-way hedge/CfD contract. This power contract would increase revenue for the nuclear power plant when electricity market prices were low (i.e., below the CfD strike price) and lower costs for electricity consumers when electricity market prices were high (i.e., above the CfD strike price).

In March 2016, the Public Utilities Commission of Ohio approved the CfD proposal.[99] A few weeks later, FERC rescinded a waiver of affiliate power sales for the new nuclear electricity CfD contract, and the CfD proposal was not implemented.[100]

### US DOE Resilience Initiative

In September 2017, the US Department of Energy (DOE) sent a Notice of Proposed Rulemaking (NOPR) to the FERC to enhance US electricity system resilience. The NOPR would have provided cost recovery for power plants that maintain 90 days of fuel at the plant site, including nuclear power plants.

This system resilience proposal would have transformed merchant nuclear power plants into regulated assets. FERC rejected the DOE Resilience NOPR.

### UK RAB Approach

The UK RAB approach would create new regulated nuclear power utilities that would invest in, own, and operate new UK nuclear power plants.[101]

The proposed UK RAB approach details are not final or approved, but the premise is that new UK nuclear power plants could be developed under a regulated asset regime like the US regulated utility approach.

# Control Negative Externalities

Another way to resolve market failure for nuclear power is to control unpriced negative externalities from other power plant technologies.

Carbon dioxide and other air pollutant emissions from combustion-based generation are a substantial issue. These emissions are unpriced negative externalities that make electricity from combustion-based generation cheaper than electricity from clean generation technologies like nuclear power.

### Carbon Tax

Carbon taxes put a price on carbon dioxide emissions from power plants by increasing the cost of fossil fuels taxed based on carbon content.

A carbon tax would increase the cost of electricity from combustion-based power plants and make electricity from clean generation technologies, like nuclear power, more competitive.

Carbon taxes are straight-forward in the traditional electricity industry approach. Carbon taxes increase the cost of electricity from combustion-based electricity generators and increase the value of clean electricity, like that from nuclear power. Carbon tax costs are reflected in the regulated utility's merit order dispatch, and the total cost of the carbon tax is recovered in consumer rates.

Carbon taxes are more complicated in electricity markets. Carbon taxes increase the marginal cost of combustion-based power plants, along with their bids into the electricity spot market. Combustion-based power plants are usually the marginal bidders in electricity markets, so higher marginal bids due to a carbon tax will also increase electricity market spot prices. Increased spot prices increase wholesale electricity costs for all users and increase revenue for all inframarginal bidders, including nuclear power plants.

Carbon taxes will increase the cost of electricity to consumers in both approaches, and if the carbon tax is large, the impact on consumers and the economy will be significant. Some carbon tax proposals call for a return of carbon tax revenue to the public to offset this negative impact on the economy (i.e., a revenue-neutral carbon tax).

The electricity industry approach matters for revenue-neutral carbon tax plans.

In the traditional approach, carbon tax costs are included in cost-based electricity rates, making it relatively easy to implement a revenue-neutral carbon tax approach.

However, it may be difficult to design and implement a revenue-neutral carbon tax in the new electricity market approach. Carbon taxes increase the electricity wholesale market price and the revenue for all generators, including inframarginal bidders that contribute no carbon tax revenue (e.g., nuclear power, hydroelectric, and renewables) and bidders that contribute lower carbon tax revenue than the marginal bidder (e.g., natural gas combined-cycle plants).

In an electricity market, a carbon tax would result in electricity cost increases that are higher than the carbon tax revenue collected. In these markets, returning all carbon tax revenue would not be enough to offset the negative impact on the economy from increased electricity costs.

In some electricity markets with a carbon tax, a windfall profit tax has been imposed on nuclear, hydroelectric, and other clean generation technology.[102] The windfall profit tax captures the financial benefit from carbon taxes to inframarginal bidders that pay no carbon taxes, including nuclear power plants. A windfall profits tax may reduce or remove the benefits to nuclear power plants from a carbon tax.

Carbon pricing may help improve nuclear power economics, but this depends on the carbon tax details, the electricity industry approach, and whether any other programs (e.g., windfall profit taxes) are used.

To take real action, nuclear power plant owners will want assurance that the government's commitment to carbon taxes is credible, that carbon taxes will be high and long-lasting, and that the government will not claw back any carbon tax benefits.[103]

### *Carbon Pricing*

Other carbon pricing approaches may also increase electricity market prices and help resolve unpriced negative externalities related to carbon emissions.

The US Regional Greenhouse Gas Initiative (RGGI) is a program for capping and gradually decreasing carbon dioxide emissions from the power sector in the Northeast and Mid-Atlantic regions. RGGI sets carbon allowances and holds auctions for these allowances, putting a price on carbon emissions.

Pennsylvania's plans to join RGGI was noted as a factor in keeping the Beaver Valley nuclear power plant from closing early in 2021.[104] However, it is important to note that Vermont and Massachusetts are RGGI members, but the Vermont Yankee and Pilgrim nuclear power plants in these states closed early. New York is also an RGGI member that found it necessary to implement ZEC payments to prevent multiple merchant nuclear power plants from closing early.

### *Regulations*

Imposing regulations to prevent negative externalities in the electricity industry might limit existing and proposed combustion-based power plants due to air emissions. Such regulations might directly remove existing combustion-based power plants and prevent the construction of new ones, which would increase the value of nuclear power.

# Pay for Nuclear Power's Positive Externalities

Compensation to nuclear power plants for public benefits they now provide without compensation can provide additional revenue to resolve nuclear power market failure.

Compensating nuclear power for positive externalities applies to both the traditional and new electricity industry approaches. Additional compensation for a regulated or government nuclear power plant may increase the value of nuclear power and lower customer rates, making nuclear power a more valuable part of the regulated or government utility generating portfolio.

Additional compensation for merchant nuclear power plants that operate in electricity markets is much more important. This additional compensation may mean the difference between profitable operation and financial losses that lead to early closure.

### *Side Markets*

Merchant nuclear power plant revenue is mostly from sales into a wholesale electricity spot market. These merchant nuclear power plants can get additional revenue from side markets outside the electricity spot market.

Capacity markets are side markets that help ensure that the required level of capacity is available to maintain system reliability. Capacity markets are intended to provide additional revenue to power plants that may not be profitable based only on spot market revenue. Capacity markets can, depending on the details, provide additional revenue for merchant nuclear power plants.

Other side market products might include zero-emissions or clean electricity, reliable base-load capacity, system reliability, and system fuel diversity. Nuclear power plants can provide these products, and establish side markets for these products might increase merchant nuclear power plant revenue.

### Power Contracts

Power contracts can provide a nuclear power plant with long-term revenue that assures operation at a profit. Examples of nuclear power plant power contracts include the HPC CfD in the UK, US merchant nuclear power plant transition PPAs, the Bruce Power Refurbishment Agreement, bilateral nuclear power contracts in Turkey, and European financial contracts.

The cost of such power contracts might be recovered from ratepayers, electricity users, or a government.

### HPC CfD

The primary incentive mechanism for the HPC project is the long-term CfD contract. The HPC power contract prices implicitly reflect the value of public goods provided by the HPC nuclear power plant that is not reflected in the UK electricity market price.

### US Merchant Nuclear Power PPAs

US merchant nuclear power plants sold by regulated utility owners usually included a transitional PPA. These transitional PPAs typically had a term that ended when the merchant nuclear power plant's original NRC operational license ended. During the term of the transitional PPA, the parties were insulated from electricity spot market prices. When the transitional PPAs ended, merchant nuclear power plants faced electricity spot market prices that were lower than expected.

There are two examples of how power contracts were used to keep US merchant nuclear plants from early closure. These include the Point Beach transition PPA, the Duane Arnold contract extension, the Ginna reliability contract, and the Millstone zero-carbon contract.

### *Point Beach*

The Point Beach nuclear power plant has two PWR units in Wisconsin that were placed into commercial operation in 1970 and 1973. These units are near the Kewaunee nuclear power plant that closed early due to financial issues.

Point Beach was built by Wisconsin Energy Corporation, a regulated utility. In 2005, Wisconsin Energy applied for and received approval for a 20-year license renewal for both units, so that new license expiration dates are in 2030 for unit 1 and 2033 for unit 2.

Wisconsin Energy sold Point Beach to FPL Energy (now NextEra Energy) on 20 Dec 2006. The sale included PPAs for the remainder of the plant's renewed operating licenses, so the PPAs expire in 2030 and 2033.

The Point Beach PPA prices were competitive at the time the PPAs were negotiated in 2006. More recently, Wisconsin Electric, the regulated counterparty to the Point Beach PPAs, noted that the PPAs are a factor in high customer rates.[105] In the December 2019 rate case for Wisconsin Energy, the utility agreed to review alternatives to the Point Beach PPA.[106]

In November 2020, NextEra Energy applied to the NRC to operate the Point Beach units for an additional 20 years (a total of 80 years), with new expiration dates of 2050 and 2053.

The key difference between Point Beach, which remains in operation, and the neighboring Kewaunee nuclear power plant, which closed early, is that the Point Beach transitional PPAs had a much longer term because the power plant was sold after the original owner had received approval for a 20-year license renewal.

### *Duane Arnold*

The Duane Arnold nuclear power plant had a PPA that would expire in 2014, but the new owner obtained NRC approval to operate until 2034. In 2013, the Iowa Utilities Board allowed Interstate Power & Light (IP&L), the buyer of power from Duane Arnold, to amend and extend the long-term power contract with Duane Arnold to cover an additional 12 years.

The state regulator approved the contract amendment because it provided benefits to IP&L's customers. In addition to the economic impact on ratepayers, the Iowa Utilities Board considered other economic benefits, including local jobs, of the Duane Arnold nuclear plant's continued operation.[107]

This renewed power contract enabled operation from 2014 until 2020 when the Duane Arnold plant was closed early due to a buy-out of the extended PPA.

### *Ginna*

In 2014, the R.E. Ginna Nuclear Power Plant (Ginna), a merchant nuclear power plant that sells power into the New York ISO wholesale electricity market, was to close early due to financial losses. The early closure of Ginna would have resulted in local/regional grid reliability issues.

New York required Ginna and Rochester Gas & Electric Corporation, a regulated electricity supplier, to buy power from the Ginna nuclear power plant to provide additional revenue to keep the plant in operation to maintain system reliability. The power contract costs were recovered from RG&E customers, who benefited from the enhanced grid reliability.

### *Millstone*

Some include Connecticut with the ZEC programs in New York, Illinois, New Jersey, and Ohio, but the Connecticut approach is slightly different.

In 2017, the Connecticut legislature authorized the state's Department of Environmental Protection to solicit zero-carbon electricity generation resources, including nuclear. The Connecticut Public Utilities Regulatory Authority (PURA) issued a decision in 2018 that categorized the Millstone nuclear power plant at risk for closure without ratepayer support. This decision allowed Millstone to participate in the state RFP for up to 12 million MWh per year of zero-carbon generation.

About half of Millstone's output cleared that auction, leading to a signed 10-year PPA for nine million MWh per year between Millstone and a load-serving electric utility

### *Bruce Power Refurbishment Agreement*

Ontario has achieved very low carbon dioxide emissions with nuclear power, even though it has an electricity market. Ontario does not rely on the electricity market to maintain the power plant fleet and deliver new power plant investments.

The Ontario electricity planning approach has been used to support significant nuclear power plant refurbishment investments. The Bruce Power nuclear plant is an example of using long-term power contracts to provide these investment incentives.

The original Bruce Power Refurbishment Implementation Agreement was signed in 2005 to support the restart of Bruce units 1 and 2.

In December 2013, the Ontario Long Term Energy Plan (LTEP) was released. A key element of the LTEP is the Refurbishment of the remaining nuclear units at the Bruce Site that are yet to be refurbished. The Refurbishment of these six units encompasses approximately 4,800 MW of nuclear capacity and billions of capital investment dollars. The Ontario Independent Energy System Operator (IESO) negotiated an agreement with Bruce Power to enable the refurbishment and continued operation of the Bruce Site consistent with the LTEP. The Amended and Restated Bruce Power Refurbishment Implementation Agreement, signed in December 2015, is the result of these negotiations.[108]

Under the December 2015 Agreement, the electricity produced by Bruce Power is purchased at a price that provides Bruce Power an opportunity to earn a negotiated Target Rate of Return on funds invested in refurbishing the Bruce Power units over the term of the Agreement (i.e., until December 2064).

Only a government could enter into a credible long-term contract to provide incentives for Bruce Power to invest substantial amounts in refurbishing the Bruce Power units to extend their life to more than 60 years.

### *Turkey Bilateral Nuclear Power contracts*

Turkey's nuclear power plant program relies on companies that build, own, and operate merchant nuclear power plants. These merchant nuclear power plants have some portion of their output covered by bilateral power contracts that provide some degree of revenue certainty.

### *Akkuyu*

Akkuyu is a four-unit nuclear power plant in southern Turkey on the Mediterranean Sea. Rosatom and its affiliated companies will invest in, build, own, and operate the Akkuyu nuclear power plant. Rosatom is investing in the Akkuyu nuclear power plant for multiple reasons, including the profits from selling electricity into the Turkish electricity market using bilateral power contracts.

Turkish Electricity Trade and Contract Corporation (TETAS) buys electricity from IPPs and government-owned power plants and sells this electricity to Turkish regional regulated electricity retail companies. TETAŞ will purchase 70% of the electricity generated by the first two units and 30% of the electricity generated by the third and fourth units in 15-year power purchase agreements at fixed prices. Additional electricity from the Akkuyu nuclear power plants will be sold in the market.

### *Sinop*

Sinop was a proposed merchant nuclear power plant in northern Turkey on the Black Sea. Sinop was a four-unit nuclear power plant developed by Mitsubishi Heavy Industries that would have used the new ATMEA-1 reactor design.

Like the Akkuyu project, the Sinop project was based on power contracts with TETAŞ. Unlike Akkuyu, the Sinop project would have had 49% ownership by the Turkish state-owned power generation company.

The Japanese sponsors abandoned the Sinop project for various reasons, including the high risk of a FOAK reactor design and higher-than-expected capital cost estimates.

## European Financial Contracts

Finnish Mankala rules allow large electricity users, both utilities and industrial companies, to cooperate in owning a nuclear power plant with full requirements power contracts.

Two European arrangements, Exeltium and Blue Sky, involved long-term power contracts between nuclear power plants and electricity-intensive industrial users.

These contracts provide industrial customers with benefits comparable with owning a nuclear power plant, including firm rights to electricity and prices based on nuclear power plant generating costs.

## Finnish Mankala Companies

Finnish Mankala law allows companies to cooperate to build, own, and operate nuclear power plants. The Olkiluoto and Hanhikivi nuclear power projects are owned by Mankala companies Teollisuuden Voima Oyj (TVO) and Fennovoima. These Mankala companies are like US electricity generation and transmission cooperatives. While US cooperatives involve tax-exempt public power entities, Finnish Mankala companies can include private companies. Finnish Mankala companies can obtain electricity from the power plants they own at cost and without taxation impacts.

A Mankala project member has, in effect, a full requirements power contract for its share of the power plant. The member gets a share of the power plant's output and pays a share of the power plant's costs.

## Exeltium

The Exeltium project was developed to provide French electricity-intensive industrial customers with electricity at a competitive and stable price. Exeltium was established to hedge the electricity prices of a group of industrial companies that were Exeltium shareholders.

Exeltium negotiated a 24-year take-or-pay power contract for 148 TWh of electricity from EDF that started in May 2010. Exeltium paid EDF for this electricity at a price linked to EDF's cost of operating its nuclear power plants, rather than electricity market prices. The deal included an upfront €1.75 billion payment to EDF financed by a mix of equity from the Exeltium shareholders and debt financing.

Exeltium shareholders received electricity at competitive and stable prices, EDF locked in a large customer, and EDF received an upfront cash payment to bolster its balance sheet.

### *Blue Sky*

Nuclear power operators Electrabel and GDF Suez agreed to sell 200 MWe of electricity from the Doel-1, Doel-2, and Tihange-1 nuclear power plants to six companies in electricity-intensive industries at the average generating cost of the nuclear power plants. The Blue Sky arrangement started in 2012 and will continue until the nuclear power plants are closed.

### *Tax Credits*

Governments might provide additional revenue to nuclear power plants by providing tax credits or preferential income tax rates for nuclear power plants. These tax credits or preferential tax rates would help compensate nuclear power plants for the positive public goods they provide.

An example of this is the electricity production tax credits in the US Energy Policy Act of 2005. This production tax credit is available for the first 6,000 MWe of advanced nuclear power that started commercial operation by the end of 2020.

In 2018, US legislation removed the requirement for 2020 commercial operation, allowing new nuclear power projects with later expected commercial operation dates (e.g., the Vogtle 3 & 4 project and the planned NuScale SMR plant in Idaho) to be eligible for production tax credits.[109]

A new PTC has been proposed in the US, with Senate Bill 4897 including a production tax credit for financially threatened merchant nuclear plants.[110] Section 301 of this draft legislation allows nuclear power plants that operate in competitive electricity markets to apply to participate in a bidding process for 2-year tax credits. The US Senate or House has not approved the legislation.

## Clean Energy Mandates

A national zero-carbon or clean energy portfolio standard is another approach that might provide nuclear power plants with additional revenue.

A clean energy mandate would require retail load-serving utilities to buy a certain percentage of their total electricity from power plants that emit no carbon dioxide (e.g., nuclear power plants). Nuclear power plants would get additional revenue from selling credits for clean or zero-carbon electricity to retail electricity companies to meet the clean energy mandate. Payments for the credits would compensate nuclear power plants for the zero-emission nuclear electricity they provide.

An example of this is the Zero Emissions Credit (ZEC) program in four US states, New York, Illinois, New Jersey, and Ohio.

### New York

The New York Clean Energy Standard (CES), adopted in August 2016, includes ZEC payments to prevent some New York merchant nuclear power plants, preventing them from closing early.[111]

Eligible nuclear power plants sell ZECs to the New York State Energy Research and Development Authority, which sells these ZECs to state-regulated retail electricity companies, and the retail electricity companies recover ZEC purchase costs from customers.

The ZEC contracts have a 12-year term with prices adjusted every two years based on the US Environmental Protection Agency's Social Cost of Carbon, revenue from RGGI, and revenue from spot and capacity markets.

Eligibility for the ZEC program is based on public necessity. New York found that the FitzPatrick, Ginna, and Nine Mile nuclear power plants in northern New York were eligible for the ZEC program. New York decided that the Indian Point nuclear power plant in southern New York state (i.e., where electricity market prices are relatively high) was not eligible.

### *Illinois*

The 2016 Illinois Future Energy Jobs Act established the ZEC program. An RFP is used to evaluate nuclear power plant eligibility based on the risk of early closure due to economic and market conditions. The Quad Cities and Clinton nuclear power plants were awarded ZECs in the first RFP held in January 2018. ZEC prices are based on the state's social cost of carbon emissions, and ratepayers will recover the cost of the ZECs from customers.

### *New Jersey*

New Jersey enacted legislation in 2018 that established a ZEC program for the state. Nuclear power plants would be eligible for ZECs if they face financial risks that might lead to early closure. New Jersey determined that the Hope Creek and Salem nuclear power plants qualified for ZEC payments, and ZEC payments of up to $300 million a year were approved in 2019. ZECs are purchased by regulated retail electric utilities, with the cost passed through to end-use electricity customers.

### *Ohio*

Ohio House Bill 6 (HB6), approved in May 2019, established the Ohio ZEC program. HB6 was developed and approved after FirstEnergy Solutions (i.e., operator of Ohio's nuclear power plants) filed for bankruptcy in 2018.

FirstEnergy argued that continued operation of the Davis-Besse and Perry nuclear power plants would save 1,400 jobs and secure a clean energy source for the state and that these two nuclear power plants would close early without additional revenue from a ZEC program.

The Ohio ZEC program provides $150 million per year to the Davis-Besse and Perry nuclear power plants, with the cost recovered from residential ratepayers. The ZEC payments allowed FirstEnergy to emerge from bankruptcy in 2020 and reverse plans to close its two Ohio nuclear power plants early.

An investigation into corruption during the HB6 approval process resulted in the arrest of Ohio legislature members in July 2020. An initiative was launched to repeal HB6 or stop the ZEC payments to the two Ohio nuclear power plants.

## Improve Electricity Market Designs

Electricity markets are working well to achieve their design objectives (e.g., low system marginal price) but are not designed to maximize public benefits.

Nuclear power and other capital-intensive electricity generation technologies are not a good fit for electricity markets.[112] Electricity markets treat electricity as a commodity product, so changing electricity spot markets to reflect non-commodity attributes of electricity from nuclear power plants may be difficult.

One idea is to improve electricity markets by recognizing different types of electricity generation sources. For example, a bifurcated electricity market might be formed. One part of the market would cover baseload electricity, and the other part of the market would balance system demand with variable renewable and combustion-based generation.[113]

## Insights

It is unlikely that nuclear power has a place in the new electricity industry approach. It is also unlikely that a private market-based approach to the nuclear power industry can deliver new nuclear power plant investment. Significant out-of-market incentives and government support are needed in both cases to maintain and build the nuclear power sector.

The case for these incentives and other government support is that nuclear power provides public goods and benefits that a market approach to electricity and nuclear power do not deliver. Making a case for a government role in the nuclear power sector to the public (i.e., the parties that receive public goods from nuclear power and pay for those public goods) is important.

A targeted set of incentives and government support may be more feasible, cost less, and have a lower risk than sweeping changes like nationalizing the nuclear power industry.  However, the targeted actions must be large enough and certain enough to convince the owners of operating nuclear power plants to keep them in operation and, even more difficult, convince investors to develop new nuclear power plants.

For merchant nuclear power plants, the timing, type, level, and funding of incentives must meet private investors' need to resolve completion risk and revenue risk before making a financial investment decision for a new merchant nuclear power project.

If a government invests in nuclear power, funding issues may be resolved, but issues related to construction, ownership, and operation must be addressed.

A caveat:  Government action is not a panacea for nuclear power. Government action may not be soon enough or large enough to resolve nuclear market failure.  And government support is strongly linked to politics, with some governments like Germany and South Korea taking action to stop nuclear power despite earlier success.

# A CALL TO ACTION

*"Mankind has been addicted to fire for over 400,000 years - and it needs an intervention."*

Mathijs Beckers - *Climate Zero Hour: Crossing the Energy Debate Divide*[114]

*"If the US keeps closing nuclear power plants and fails to build new ones, we will cede our ability to compete with the Russians and Chinese in building new nuclear power plants abroad, which will undermine national security and good industrial jobs at home."*

Michael Shellenberger - *I Was Invited to Testify on Energy Policy. Then Democrats Didn't Let Me Speak*[115]

Nuclear power is necessary for a zero-emission electricity sector.

IPCC 1.5°C pathways call for nuclear power plant capacity to increase from the current 392 MWe to a much higher level, ranging from 960 to 2,300 GWe, by 2050.[116] And even more new nuclear power will be needed to replace existing nuclear power plant plants that will close by 2050. A massive nuclear power build program is needed.

A market-based approach to nuclear power will not deliver enough new nuclear capacity to replace units that will close, much less to meet the need for new nuclear power capacity. Only government-led nuclear power plant build programs can deliver this new nuclear power plant capacity.

The highest priority is preventing the early closure of operating nuclear power plants. The next priority is to move away from a market approach to nuclear power, then put a government-led nuclear power build program in place.

The issues in this book are seen in multiple countries.

- The UK has strong support for nuclear power from the government and the public. New nuclear power plants are needed to replace retiring AGR units and meet climate goals, but face issues in the UK market-based electricity industry. The UK is considering a government equity role in new merchant nuclear power plant projects.

- The US faces the early closure of more merchant nuclear power plants. The new Biden administration has goals to decarbonize the US electricity sector by 2035 but the details for nuclear power are not clear. Legislation to provide tax credits to threatened merchant nuclear power plants is under review, but much more needs to be done.

- Japan is implementing market reforms in the electricity sector while ensuring that nuclear power remains viable and trying to avoid nuclear power market failure.

- Australia is considering nuclear power as a zero-carbon generation option at the same time as it considers electricity market reforms to address, among other things, the high penetration of renewable generation.

Countries with a market approach to the electricity and nuclear power industry may see existing nuclear power plants closed early, with no investment in new nuclear power plants. These countries may not have a nuclear power industry in the long-term.

Countries with a traditional electricity sector and strong government support for nuclear power can resolve nuclear power market failure and facilitate a strong nuclear power industry.

The future of the nuclear power industry will be defined by countries that support and build nuclear power.

# Market Failure

# ABOUT THE AUTHOR

Edward Kee is the CEO, Founder, and principal consultant of Nuclear Economics Consulting Group (NECG). He is an expert on nuclear power economics and provides strategic and economic advice to companies and governments on nuclear power and electricity industry issues. He has testified as an expert witness in US and international legal and arbitration cases.

The International Atomic Energy Agency (IAEA), the International Framework for Nuclear Energy Cooperation (IFNEC), and the US Civil Nuclear Trade Advisory Committee (CINTAC) have recognized Mr. Kee as a nuclear power industry expert.

Before founding NECG, he held senior consulting positions at NERA Economic Consulting, CRA International, PA Consulting Group, Putnam, Hayes & Bartlett, and McKinsey & Company. Earlier, he was a merchant power plant developer and a nuclear power plant engineer in the US Navy.

He writes and publishes NECG Commentaries on nuclear economics issues.

Edward has published articles on nuclear power and the electricity industry in the *Wall Street Journal, World Nuclear News, Nuclear Engineering International, ANS Nuclear News, Nuclear power International, the Bulletin of the Atomic Scientists, The Electricity Journal,* and *Public Utilities Fortnightly.*

He has taught courses on nuclear economics and related matters for the International Atomic Energy Agency and has been a guest lecturer for university courses, client workshops, and board meetings.

Edward Kee has an MBA from Harvard University and a B.S. in Systems Engineering (Distinction, Trident Scholar, Colt's Award) from the US Naval Academy.

He completed the US Navy nuclear power training program before his assignment to the USS Carl Vinson (CVN-70) nuclear-powered aircraft carrier during construction and was qualified to serve as chief engineering officer on Nimitz-class nuclear aircraft carriers.

More information on Mr. Kee is at https://nuclear-economics.com/edward-kee/.

# NOTES

[1]    David Roberts, *How to save the failing nuclear power plants that generate half of America's clean electricity,* VOX, 11 May 2018, https://www.vox.com/energy-and-environment/2018/5/10/17334474/nuclear-power-renewables-plants-retirements-us.

[2]    James Lovelock, *Nuclear Energy for the 21st Century*, Paris Speech, 21-22 March 2005, http://www.jameslovelock.org/nuclear-energy-for-the-21st-century/.

[3]    Ulrich Becker, Bruno Coppi, Eric Cosman, Peter Demos, Arthur Kerman, and Richard Milner, *A Perspective on the Future Energy Supply of the United States: The Urgent Need for Increased Nuclear Power*, *MIT Faculty Newsletter* Vol. XXI, No.2, November / December 2008. http://web.mit.edu/fnl/volume/212/milner.html.

[4]    World Nuclear Association, World Nuclear Performance Report 2020, https://www.world-nuclear.org/our-association/publications/global-trends-reports/world-nuclear-performance-report.aspx

[5]    *The Full Costs of Electricity Provision*, Nuclear Energy Agency, 2018, https://doi.org/10.1787/9789264303119-en.

[6]    John R. Mullin and Zenia Kotval, *The Closing of Yankee Rowe Nuclear Power Plant: The Impact on a New England Community*, UMass Amherst Landscape Architecture & Regional Planning Faculty Publication Series, October 1997, https://scholarworks.umass.edu/larp_faculty_pubs/25/.

[7]    Samuel C. Johnson, Dimitri J. Papageorgiou, Dharik S. Mallapragada, Thomas A. Deetjen, Joshua D. Rhodes, and Michael E. Webber; *Evaluating rotational inertia as a component of grid reliability with high penetrations of variable renewable energy*, Energy, Vol 180, 1 August 2019, Pages 258-271, https://www.sciencedirect.com/science/article/pii/S0360544219308564.

[8]    Edward Kee, *NECG Commentary #1 – Long-Term Assets in a Short-Term World*, 31 August 2014, https://nuclear-economics.com/nuclear-power-plants/.

[9]    Andrew Kadak, *A Comparison of Advanced Nuclear Technologies*, Columbia SIPA Center on Global Energy Policy, March 2017, http://energypolicy.columbia.edu/sites/default/files/A%20Comparison%20of%20Nuclear%20Technologies%20033017.pdf.

[10]    International Atomic Energy Association, Power Reactor Information System, accessed 30 December 2020, https://pris.iaea.org/PRIS/WorldStatistics/OperationalReactorsByType.aspx.

[11]    International Atomic Energy Association, Power Reactor Information System, accessed 30 December 2020, https://pris.iaea.org/PRIS/WorldStatistics/OperationalReactorsByType.aspx.

[12]    International Atomic Energy Association, Power Reactor Information System, accessed 30 December 2020, https://pris.iaea.org/PRIS/WorldStatistics/OperationalReactorsByType.aspx.

[13]    Heavy water reactors use heavy water as a primary coolant and moderator. Heavy water contains a higher-than-normal concentration of heavier hydrogen isotopes.

[14]    International Atomic Energy Association, Power Reactor Information System, accessed 30 December 2020, https://pris.iaea.org/PRIS/WorldStatistics/OperationalReactorsByType.aspx.

[15]    Reinberger D., Ajanovic A., and Haas R., *The Technological Development of Different Generations and Reactor Concepts*, The Technological and Economic Future of Nuclear Power, Energy Policy and Climate Protection, 2019, https://doi.org/10.1007/978-3-658-25987-7_11.

[16]    Stephen M. Goldberg and Robert Rosner, *Nuclear Reactors: Generation to Generation*, American Academy of Arts and Sciences, 2011, https://www.amacad.org/publication/nuclear-reactors-generation-generation.

[17]    US Department of Energy, *What Is a Nuclear Microreactor?* 23 October 2018, https://www.energy.gov/ne/articles/what-nuclear-microreactor.

[18]    US Nuclear Regulatory Commission, *NRC mission*, "The NRC licenses and regulates the Nation's civilian use of radioactive materials to provide reasonable assurance of adequate protection of public health and safety and to promote the common defense and security and to protect the environment." https://www.nrc.gov/about-nrc.html

[19]    Will Davis, *Nuclear power plant Costs – A Look Back and Ahead,* ANS Nuclear Café, 16 February 2016; http://ansnuclearcafe.org/2016/02/16/nuclear-plant-cost-escalation-a-look-back-and-ahead/.

[20]    Edward Kee, *NECG Commentary #2, Nuclear Power & Short-Run Marginal Cost*, 1 October 2014, https://nuclear-economics.com/nuclear-power-short-run-marginal-cost/.

21    The US nuclear waste fee required operators of nuclear power plants to pay a tenth of a cent per kilowatt-hour to the government in return for US DOE taking responsibility for spent nuclear fuel, with the collection of this fee stopped in 2014.

22    Edward Kee, *NECG Commentary #3 - Nuclear Base Load*, 3 November 2014, https://nuclear-economics.com/nuclear-base-load/.

23    Laurent Pouret and William Nuttall, *Can Nuclear Power be Flexible?*, *University of Cambridge, Energy Policy Research Group*, EPRG 0710, 21 January 2014, https://www.eprg.group.cam.ac.uk/eprg-0710/.

24    Edward Kee, *NECG Commentary #12 - Nuclear Flexibility*, 24 September 2015, https://nuclear-economics.com/12-nuclear-flexibility/.

25    *Refurbishment Agreement*, Bruce Power, 2015, https://www.brucepower.com/life-extension-program-mcr-project/refurbishment-agreement/.

26    Alexey Lokhov, *Technical and Economic Aspects of Load Following with Nuclear Power Plants*, Nuclear Energy Agency, June 2011, http://www.oecd-nea.org/ndd/reports/2011/load-following-npp.pdf.

27    D.T. Ingersoll, C. Colbert, Z. Houghton, R. Snuggerud, J.W. Gaston, and M. Empey; *Can Nuclear Power and Renewables be Friends?*, Proceedings of ICAPP 2015, 3-6 May 2015.

28    *EDF to Maintain Sizewell B at Reduced Capacity,* Nuclear Street News, 13 May 2020, https://nuclearstreet.com/nuclear_power_industry_news/b/nuclear_power_news/archive/2020/05/13/edf-to-maintain-sizewell-b-at-reduced-capacity-05132020.

29    Rod Adams, *Why don't we mothball shutdown nuclear power plants?*, ANS Nuclear Café, 3 September 2013; http://ansnuclearcafe.org/2013/09/03/why-dont-we-mothball-nuclear-plants/.

30    Jonathan Kahn, *Keep HOPE Alive: Updating the Prudent Investment Standard for Allocating Nuclear Plant Cancellation Costs*, Mitchell Hamline School of Law, Faculty Scholarship Paper 399, 22 Fordham Environmental Law Review 43, 2010, http://open.mitchellhamline.edu/facsch/399.

31    Perry, Robert L., Arthur J. Alexander, Wendy Allen, Peter DeLeon, Arturo Gandara, W. E. Mooz, Elizabeth S. Rolph, Sidney Siegel, and Kenneth A. Solomon, *Development and Commercialization of the Light Water Reactor, 1946-1976*, RAND Corporation, 1977. https://www.rand.org/pubs/reports/R2180.html.

32    Alexis C. Madrigal, *The Nuclear Breakthrough That Wasn't, The Atlantic*, 22 March 2011, https://www.theatlantic.com/technology/archive/2011/03/the-nuclear-breakthrough-that-wasnt/72816/.

33    Geert de Clercq, *UPDATE 2 - Rescued Areva faces uncertain future as nuclear fuel group*, Reuters, 4 June 2015, https://www.reuters.com/article/areva-edf/update-2-rescued-areva-faces-uncertain-future-as-nuclear-fuel-group-idUSL5N0YQ13720150604.

34    H. Stuart Burness, W. David Montgomery, and James Quirk, *The Turnkey Era in Nuclear Power*, *Land Economics*, Vol. 56 No. 2, May 1980, p. 195-196; https://www.jstor.org/stable/3145862?seq=1.

35    Will Davis, *Nuclear power plant Costs – A Look Back and Ahead,* ANS Nuclear Café, 16 February 2016; http://ansnuclearcafe.org/2016/02/16/nuclear-plant-cost-escalation-a-look-back-and-ahead/.

36    Richard Milne and David Keohane, *Areva and Siemens settle Finland nuclear power plant dispute*, *Financial Times*, 11 March 2018, https://www.ft.com/content/dda39a0c-256e-11e8-b27e-cc62a39d57a0 (behind paywall).

37    Arizona Nuclear Power Project, Participation Agreement, 23 August 1973, https://www.sec.gov/Archives/edgar/data/31978/000003197818000011/eeex_1001aznuclear power82373.htm.

38    David Fishman, Quiet but not dead – China's Nuclear Program now Poised to Swing Back into Full Gear, The Lantau Group, November 2019, https://www.lantaugroup.com/publications/display/Quiet-But-Not-Dead---China-s-Nuclear-Program-Now-Poised-to-Swing-Back-Into-Full-Gear.

39    Ian Bremmer, *The End of the Free Market*, Portfolio, 2010, ISBN: 978-1591843016.

40    Edward Kee, *Can nuclear succeed in liberalized power markets? World Nuclear News Viewpoint*, 4 February 2015, http://www.world-nuclear-news.org/V-Can-nuclear-succeed-in-liberalized-power-markets-0420152.html.

41    NECG Recommended Reading list, https://nuclear-economics.com/recommended-reading/, has good sources on the electricity industry and its reform, especially *Markets for Power* by Paul L Joskow and Richard Schmalensee; *The Economics of Regulation: Principles and Institutions* by Alfred E. Kahn; *Energy Companies and Market Reform: How Deregulation Went Wrong* by Jeremiah Lambert; *Privatization, Restructuring, and Regulation of Network Utilities (Walras-Pareto Lectures)* by David M Newbery; and *Power System Economics: Designing Markets for Electricity* by Steven Stoft.

42    Severin Borenstein and James Bushnell, *The U.S. Electricity Industry after 20 Years of Restructuring*, *Annual Review of Economics*, Vol. 7, August 2015, pages 437-463; https://www.annualreviews.org/doi/abs/10.1146/annurev-economics-080614-115630.

43    Lester Lave, Jay Apt, and Seth Blumsack, *Deregulation / Restructuring Part I: Reregulation will not fix the problems*, *The Electricity Journal*, Volume 20, Issue 8, October 2007, https://www.sciencedirect.com/science/article/abs/pii/S1040619007001042.

44    Edward Kee, *Privatization and deregulation, moving from monopolies to* markets, PA Consulting Group Viewpoint on industry restructuring, 2002, https://nuclear-economics.com/wp-content/uploads/2016/01/2002-01-01-Monopolies-to-Markets-PA-Viewpoint-on-industry-restructuring-EDK.pdf.

45    Phillip F. Schewe; *The Grid: A Journey Through the Heart of Our Electrified World*, Washington, DC; Joseph Henry Press, 2007, https://doi.org/10.17226/11735.

46    Electricity storage, in the form of large pumped-storage hydroelectric facility and smaller battery, flywheel, and other technology, is present in limited amounts in some systems. System dispatch includes management of input to and output from any electricity storage devices in the system.

47    Edward Kee, *NECG Commentary #2 - Nuclear Power & Short-Run Marginal Cost*, 1 October 2014, https://nuclear-economics.com/nuclear-power-short-run-marginal-cost/.

48    Paul L Joskow and Richard Schmalensee, *Markets for Power, An Analysis of Electric Utility Deregulation*, MIT Press, ISBN: 9780262100281, 1983.

49    Carlos Waters, *This "duck curve" is solar energy's greatest challenge*, VOX, 9 May 2018, https://www.vox.com/2018/5/9/17336330/duck-curve-solar-energy-supply-demand-problem-caiso-nrel.

50    Giles Parkinson, *Solar meets 100 per cent of South Australia demand for first time*, Renew Economy, 12 October 2020, https://reneweconomy.com.au/solar-meets-100-per-cent-of-south-australia-demand-for-first-time-78279/.

51    Arturo Cifuentes and David Espinoza, *Infrastructure investing and the peril of discounted cash flow: valuation techniques remain anchored in arcane ideas*, Financial Times, Opinion Markets Insight; 3 November 2016; https://www.ft.com/content/c9257c6c-a0db-11e6-891e-abe238dee8e2 (behind paywall).

52    *New nuclear 'the most efficient way' to decarbonise grids, NNWI report finds*, World Nuclear News, 22 October 2020, https://world-nuclear-news.org/Articles/New-nuclear-the-most-efficient-way-to-decarbonise.

53    William W. Hogan, *Market Design Practices: Which ones are Best? [In My View]*, IEEE Power and Energy Magazine, Volume 17, Issue 1, January-February 2019, https://ieeexplore.ieee.org/document/8606530.

54    Gordon Leslie, David Stern, Akshay Shanker, and Michael Hogan; *Designing electricity markets for high penetrations of zero or low marginal cost intermittent energy sources;* The Electricity Journal, Volume 33, Issue 9, November 2020, 106847, https://www.sciencedirect.com/science/article/abs/pii/S1040619020301391?via%3Dihub.

55    Edward Kee, *NECG Commentary #14 - Market Failure and Nuclear Power*, 24 June 2016, https://nuclear-economics.com/14-market-failure/.

56    *Energy Policies of IEA Countries: The United States 2014 Review*, International Energy Agency, 2014, https://webstore.iea.org/energy-policies-of-iea-countries-the-united-states-2014-review.

57    Edward Kee, *NECG Commentary #14 - Market Failure and Nuclear Power*, 24 June 2016, https://nuclear-economics.com/14-market-failure/.

58    Edward Kee, *Market Failure and Nuclear Power*, Bulletin of the Atomic Scientists, 4 August 2016. https://thebulletin.org/%E2%80%9Cmarket-failure%E2%80%9D-and-nuclear-power9703.

59    *Nuclear Power in a Clean Energy System,* International Energy Agency, Fuel Report, May 2019, https://www.iea.org/reports/nuclear-power-in-a-clean-energy-system.

60    World Nuclear Association, *World Nuclear Performance Report 2020,* Page 59, Section 4, Director General's Concluding Remarks, August 2020, https://www.world-nuclear.org/our-association/publications/global-trends-reports/world-nuclear-performance-report.aspx.

61    Idaho National Laboratory, Light Water Reactor Sustainability Program, *Economic and Market Challenges Facing the U.S. Nuclear Commercial Fleet – Cost and Revenue Study*; INL/EXT-17-42944, September 2017, https://nuclear-economics.com/wp-content/uploads/2017/10/2017-09-Market-Challenges-for-Nuclear-Fleet-ESSAI-Study.pdf.

62    Steve Clemmer, Jeremy Richardson, Sandra Sattler, and Dave Lochbaum, *The Nuclear Power Dilemma*, Union of Concerned Scientists, 9 October 2018, https://www.ucsusa.org/resources/nuclear-power-dilemma.

63    Congressional Research Service, *Nuclear Power: Outlook for New U.S. Reactors*, RL3342, 9 March 2007, https://www.everycrsreport.com/reports/RL33442.html#_Toc217382792.

64    Matthew L. Wald, *Oregon Reactor to be Shut Down*, New York Times, 11 August 1992, https://www.nytimes.com/1992/08/11/us/oregon-reactor-to-be-shut-down.html (behind paywall).

65    Robert Davis and Peter Kendall, *ComEd Closing Zion Nuclear Power Plant*, Chicago Tribune, 15 January 1998, https://www.chicagotribune.com/news/ct-xpm-1998-01-15-9801160672-story.html.

66    *Southern California Edison Announces Plans to Retire San Onofre Nuclear Generating Station*, Edison International News Release, 7 June 2013, https://newsroom.edison.com/releases/southern-california-edison-announces-plans-to-retire-san-onofre-nuclear-generating-station.

67    Matthew Wald, *As Price of Nuclear Energy Drops, a Wisconsin Plant is Shut*, New York Times, 7 May 2013, https://www.nytimes.com/2013/05/08/business/energy-environment/kewaunee-nuclear-power-plant-shuts-down.html (behind paywall).

68    Wayne Parry, *Oyster Creek, oldest nuke plant in the U.S., closing a year ahead of schedule,* northjersey.com, 2 February 2018, https://www.northjersey.com/story/news/new-jersey/2018/02/02/oyster-creek-oldest-nuke-plant-u-s-closing-year-ahead-schedule/301448002/.

69    Steve Adams, *Poll: NRC votes to renew Pilgrim nuclear power plant's license*, The Patriot Ledger, 25 May 2012, https://www.patriotledger.com/x1832947103/License-renewal-to-come-for-Plymouth-Nuclear-Power-Station.

70    *Iowa's lone nuclear plant to close in 2020 under revised PPA*, American Public Power Association, 30 July 2018, https://www.publicpower.org/periodical/article/iowas-lone-nuclear-plant-close-2020-under-revised-ppa.

71  *Exelon Generation to Retire Illinois' Byron and Dresden Nuclear Plants in 2021*, Exelon Newsroom, 27 August 2020, *https://www.exeloncorp.com/newsroom/exelon-generation-to-retire-illinois%E2%80%99-byron-and-dresden-nuclear-plants-in-2021*.

72  *Joint Proposal*, Pacific Gas & Electric, 20 June 2016, https://www.pge.com/en_US/safety/how-the-system-works/diablo-canyon-power-plant/joint-proposal.page.

73  *Exelon Generation to Retire Illinois' Byron and Dresden Nuclear Plants in 2021*, Exelon Newsroom, 27 August 2020, *https://www.exeloncorp.com/newsroom/exelon-generation-to-retire-illinois%E2%80%99-byron-and-dresden-nuclear-plants-in-2021*.

74  Jeffrey Tomich and Arianna Skibell, *Deadlines loom for states mulling exit from FERC grid order*, E&E News, 1 June 2020, https://www.eenews.net/stories/1063286497.

75  Anya Litvak and Laura Legere, *Beaver Valley nuclear plant will remain open past 2021, owner says*, Pittsburgh Post-Gazette, 13 March 2020, https://www.post-gazette.com/business/powersource/2020/03/13/Beaver-Valley-nuclear-plant-remain-open-past-2021-Shippingport-Energy-Harbor-FirstEnergy/stories/202003130149.

76  Holly Watt, *Hinkley Point: the 'dreadful deal' behind the world's most expensive power plant*, The Long Read, *The Guardian*, 21 December 2017, https://www.theguardian.com/news/2017/dec/21/hinkley-point-c-dreadful-deal-behind-worlds-most-expensive-power-plant.

77  Simon Taylor, *Privatisation and Financial Collapse in the Nuclear Industry, The origins and causes of the British Energy crisis of 2002*, Routledge, 14 August 2007, ISBN: 978-0415431750.

78  Simon Taylor, *The Fall and Rise of Nuclear Power in Britain, A History*, UIT, 2 March 2016, ISBN: 9781906860318.

79  Graham Shuttleworth and Sean Gammons, *Why the UK's Proposed Reform of Electricity Markets Needs More Rational Analysis, and Less Wishful Thinking*, NERA Energy Market Insights, 25 January 2011, https://www.nera.com/content/dam/nera/publications/archive2/NL_EMI_0111.pdf.

80  *Hinkley Point C contract terms,* World Nuclear News, 8 October 2014, http://www.world-nuclear-news.org/NP-Hinkley-Point-C-contract-terms-08101401.html.

81  *UK government considers acquiring equity in new nuclear plants,* Power Technology, 7 October 2020, https://www.power-technology.com/news/uk-consider-acquire-equity-stake-new-nuclear-power-plants/.

82  Edward Kee, Ruediger Koenig, Paul Murphy, and Xavier Rollat; *NECG Commentary #30 - UK RAB Model;* 14 October 2019, https://nuclear-economics.com/30-uk-rab-model/.

83   https://www.gov.uk/government/consultations/regulated-asset-base-rab-model-for-nuclear.

84  https://www.gov.uk/government/publications/energy-white-paper-powering-our-net-zero-future.

85    *Ontario's Nuclear Advantage*, World Nuclear News, 28 February 2018, https://world-nuclear-news.org/Articles/Ontario-s-nuclear-advantage.

86    *Progress Report on Contracted Electricity Supply, Q1-2019*, Ontario Independent Electricity System Operator, 2019.

87    *Creating the Electricity Market of Tomorrow*, Ontario's Power System, Independent Electricity System Operator, 2020, http://www.ieso.ca/Learn/Ontario-Power-System/Electricity-Market-of-Tomorrow.

88    Jon Palfreman, *Why the French Like Nuclear Energy*, Frontline, PBS, 21 October 2008, http://www.pbs.org/wgbh/pages/frontline/shows/reaction/readings/french.html.

89    *Energy, Electricity and Nuclear Power Estimates for the Period up to 2050, 40th edition*, IAEA RDS-1, 2020, https://www.iaea.org/publications/14786/energy-electricity-and-nuclear-power-estimates-for-the-period-up-to-2050.

90    *France's Fessenheim-2 closes permanently,* American Nuclear Society Newswire, 1 July 2020, https://www.ans.org/news/article-310/frances-fessenheim2-closes-permanently/.

91    Mark Hibbs, The Future of Nuclear Power in China, Online: Carnegie Endowment for International Peace, 2018, https://carnegieendowment.org/2018/05/14/future-of-nuclear-power-in-china-introduction-pub-76312.

92    *James Lovelock: Nuclear power is the only green solution*, Independent, 24 May 2004, https://www.independent.co.uk/voices/commentators/james-lovelock-nuclear-power-is-the-only-green-solution-564446.html.

93    Nuclear In the States Toolkit, Policy Options for states considering the sole of nuclear power in their energy mix, Version 2.0, ANS Special Committee on Nuclear in the States, June 2016, http://nuclearconnect.org/wp-content/uploads/2016/02/ANS-NIS-Toolkit-V2.pdf.

94    *Government and Nuclear Energy*, NEA No. 5270, Nuclear Energy Agency, 2004; https://www.oecd-nea.org/ndd/pubs/2004/5270-government-nuclear-energy.pdf.

95    Edward Kee and Elise Zoli, *Rescuing U.S. Merchant Nuclear Power: Advancing National Security, Economic, Energy, and Environmental Imperatives*, The Electricity Journal, April 2014, http://nuclear-economics.com/?attachment_id=364.

96    *UK govt mulls buying stakes in nuclear plants, minister says,* Renewables Now, *7 October 2020,* https://renewablesnow.com/news/uk-govt-mulls-buying-stakes-in-nuclear-plants-minister-says-report-716326/.

97    Edward Kee, Ruediger Koenig, Paul Murphy, and Xavier Rollat; *NECG Commentary #30 - UK RAB Model;* 14 October 2019; https://nuclear-economics.com/30-uk-rab-model/.

98    Michael Shellenberger, *Don't Let China Steal the Global Nuclear-Power Industry*, New York Post, Opinion, 17 August 2020, https://www.manhattan-institute.org/dont-let-china-steal-the-global-nuclear-power-industry.

99    Public Utilities Commission of Ohio, Docket 14-1297-EL-SSO, 31 March 2016, http://dis.puc.state.oh.us/TiffToPDf/A1001001A16C31B41521H01842.pdf.

100    U.S. Federal Energy Regulatory Commission, Docket No. EL16-34-000, 27 April 2016, http://elibrary.ferc.gov/idmws/file_list.asp?accession_num=20160427-3051.

101    Edward Kee, Ruediger Koenig, Paul Murphy, and Xavier Rollat; NECG Commentary #30 - *UK RAB Model;* 14 October 2019; https://nuclear-economics.com/30-uk-rab-model/.

102    *Finland to Tax Nuclear, Hydropower to cut 'Windfall' Utility Profits*, Power Magazine, 7 April 2009, https://www.powermag.com/finland-to-tax-nuclear-hydropower-to-cut-windfall-utility-profits/.

103    Edward Kee, *Carbon pricing not enough to help nuclear power*, World Nuclear News, Perspective, 8 June 2016, http://www.world-nuclear-news.org/V-Carbon-pricing-not-enough-to-help-nuclear-power-10061601.html.

104    Anya Litvak and Laura Legere, *Beaver Valley nuclear plant will remain open past 2021, owner says*, Pittsburgh Post-Gazette, 13 March 2020, https://www.post-gazette.com/business/powersource/2020/03/13/Beaver-Valley-nuclear-plant-remain-open-past-2021-Shippingport-Energy-Harbor-FirstEnergy/stories/202003130149.

105    https://lacrossetribune.com/news/state-and-regional/point-beach-owner-seeks-to-run-wisconsins-last-nuclear-plant-for-80-years/article_c11426fc-11cb-589d-a37e-84141baab368.html.

106    Public Service Commission of Wisconsin, Joint Application of Wisconsin Electric Power Company and Wisconsin Gas LLC for Authority to Adjust Electric, Natural Gas, and Steam Rates, 5-UR-109, PSC Ref#381305, 19 December 2019.

107    State of Iowa, Department of Commerce, Utilities Board; *In Re: Interstate Power and Light Company and FPL Energy Duane Arnold, LLC*; Docket Nos. SPU-2005-0015 and TF-2012-0577; 31 January 2013.

108    *Refurbishment Agreement*, Bruce Power, 2015, https://www.brucepower.com/life-extension-program-mcr-project/refurbishment-agreement/.

109    *USA extends nuclear tax credit deadline,* World Nuclear News, 12 February 2018, https://www.world-nuclear-news.org/NP-USA-extends-nuclear-tax-credit-deadline-1202187.html.

110    https://www.epw.senate.gov/public/index.cfm/2020/11/senators-introduce-bipartisan-legislation-to-revitalize-america-s-nuclear-infrastructure.

111    McDermott Will & Emery, *NY Creates New Emissions Credit for Nuclear Plants*, Energy Business Law, 20 September 2016, https://www.energybusinesslaw.com/2016/09/articles/environmental/ny-creates-new-emissions-credit-for-nuclear-plants/.

112    Edward Kee, *NECG Commentary #1, Nuclear Power Plants – Long-Term Assets in a Short-Term World*, 31 August 2014, http://nuclear-economics.com/nuclear-power-plants/.

[113]     Xavier Rollat, *NECG Commentary #17 - Better Market Design*, 5 April 2017,
         https://nuclear-economics.com/17-better-market-design/.

[114]     Mathijs Beckers, *Climate Zero Hour*, ISBN: 978-1983589621, 1 January 2018.

[115]     Michel Shellenberger, *I was invited to Testify on Energy Policy. Then Democrats Didn't Let
         Me Speak,* Quillette, 29 July 2020, https://quillette.com/2020/07/29/why-democrats-are-
         trying-to-shut-me-up-about-climate-change-and-renewables/.

[116]     *Climate Change and Nuclear Power 2020*, IAEA, STI/PUB/1911, September 2020.